IT'S ABOUT
TIME!

Overdoer

Perfectionist

Dreamer

Crisis-Maker

Defier

Worrier

Dr. Linda Sapadin

with Jack Maguire

IT'S ABOUT TIME!

The Six Styles of Procrastination and How to Overcome Them

VIKING

VIKING
Published by the Penguin Group
Penguin Books USA Inc., 375 Hudson Street,
New York, New York 10014, U.S.A.
Penguin Books Ltd, 27 Wrights Lane, London W8 5TZ, England
Penguin Books Australia Ltd, Ringwood, Victoria, Australia
Penguin Books Canada Ltd, 10 Alcorn Avenue,
Toronto, Ontario, Canada M4V 3B2
Penguin Books (N.Z.) Ltd, 182–190 Wairau Road,
Auckland 10, New Zealand

Penguin Books Ltd, Registered Offices:
Harmondsworth, Middlesex, England

First published in 1996 by Viking Penguin,
a division of Penguin Books USA Inc.

1   3   5   7   9   10   8   6   4   2

PUBLISHER'S NOTE
The individuals described in this book have been rendered as compos-
ites of more than one real person. The actions and statements ascribed
to such an individual are a composite of the actions and statements of
the persons on whom that individual is based.

LIBRARY OF CONGRESS CATALOGING IN PUBLICATION DATA
Sapadin, Linda.
It's about time! : the six styles of procrastination and how to
overcome them / by Linda Sapadin with Jack Maguire.
p.   cm.
ISBN 0–670–85873–0 (alk. paper)
1. Procrastination. 2. Typology (Psychology)
I. Maguire, Jack, 1945–   .   II. Title.
BF637.P76S27   1996
155.2'32—dc20   95–48771

This book is printed on acid-free paper.
∞

Printed in the United States of America
Set in Bodoni Book • Designed by Francesca Belanger
Illustrations by Mark Rosenthal

To
my husband, Ron, and my sons,
Brian, Glenn, and Daniel,
for their love, support,
and inspiration

Acknowledgments

This is my first book. As such, I needed to learn a lot about *how* to get a book published so that I could move from "a good idea" to "the book is in print!" During this long process, it helps a lot be nourished and encouraged by people who believe in you. I have many of those people in my life, and it is my delight to acknowledge their contribution.

My greatest thanks and gratitude go to my husband, Ron Goodrich. He is not only a gifted and creative psychologist but also a loving and nurturing human being. When we were married, thirteen years ago, he promised me

> A beautiful, free and intimate space
> With you in the center, a smile on your face.

You have kept your promise, Ron, giving me all the space I need to grow, and even more:

> Our space together is cozy inside,
> And you can sense along with the free
> A home, belonging, and intimacy
> And you can know with all of your heart
> That this space is yours 'til death do us part.

With nurturance like this, is it any wonder that my creative spirit has continued to flourish? In addition to the above, Ron, I want you to know how much I appreciate your unflagging calm and reassurance. No problem seems so difficult or complex, because you are there to listen and offer me your good judgment. This is a better book because of your ideas, your insights, your editing.

I take tremendous pride and enjoyment from giving birth to this book. And yet, these emotions are minuscule when I compare them with the very deep pleasure I experience from being a mom to three of the most beautiful people I know. My sons, Brian, Glenn, and Daniel, each in his unique way, have been the source of my courage to live life creatively rather than safely.

Brian, your enthusiasm and willingness to "go for it" are a constant source of inspiration for me. Glenn, your imaginative spirit and wacky sense of humor are a wonderful source of enrichment for me. And, a special thanks for creating the book's title, *It's About Time!* Daniel, your sensibility and sensitivity are a winning combination that I constantly admire and learn from. Being a part of your interesting lives, my sons, from the beginning to this very moment, has been my privilege.

My thanks to my sister, Ruth, and my brother, Bob. We have been through much together in this journey of life. It's always great to celebrate the joys and triumphs with you!

To Jack Maguire, my co-writer, my deepest thanks. Together, we made it happen and in such a pleasant way! It's been a great experience. You were there to assist me in bringing my ideas to life, in addition to generating your own creative spin to the project. I appreciate it all.

To Faith Hamlin, my agent, thanks for receiving my initial proposal with a "Yes, and," not a "Yes, but." Your response encouraged me to rewrite the proposal, and as they say, the rest is history. Faith, your vision, faith, and work on my behalf are fully appreciated.

To Jane von Mehren, my editor, thanks for putting your support and enthusiasm behind this book. Your editorial input and gentle and reassuring manner have meant so much to me. And thanks to Beena Kamlani, whose many editorial changes improved the flow and clarity of the final manuscript.

In the early stages of this project, I was encouraged by several people who provided me with direction and positive energy. Thanks, Gloria Rosenthal, for your never-ending optimism and exuberance. Thanks, Ellen McGrath, for your guidance and introduction to my agent, Faith. Thanks, Beth Sherman, for your input during the early stages of the manuscript. Thanks, Marilyn Goldstein, for your excitement about the book before the proposal was even accepted. Thanks, Sheila Peck, for your "get-up-and-go" philosophy, which created many fertile projects for us to grow.

Finally, thanks to the men and women who willingly shared their stories with me, both patients and interviewees. It takes courage and integrity to tell your stories as you did. Respecting your confidentiality, I have altered identifying information and in some situations, have combined the experiences of several people's stories.

Contents

Chapter 1

How Do You
Procrastinate?

Perfectionist

Overdoer

Dreamer

Crisis-Maker

Defier

Worrier

"It drives me crazy!" Andy cried. For six years, he had been an assistant manager for an insurance firm, and most of that time he had yearned for a better job. When he first consulted me for psychotherapy, he agonized over his career misfortunes: "I never seem to get a break, and I can't understand why. It makes me furious sometimes, just thinking about it!"

Soon afterward, Andy's company offered to send him to executive development seminars, and he was very pleased. "This could be my way out of a dead-end job!" he confided. I waited for weeks to hear more about the seminars, but he didn't mention them. Finally, I brought up the subject myself. He shrugged and said, "Oh, them! I went for a while, but I didn't have the time to keep up with all the reading. Then, with one thing and another, I started missing some classes. Before long, I'd fallen too far behind to go back."

Maureen, an emergency room nurse, had only recently begun to tire of her job when she became my client. "I'm burned out," she declared. "I want to do something different, something more stimulating for my mind and less hectic for my body."

Following through with her idea, Maureen started researching job opportunities in medical publications. She pressed for any interview she could get and eventually spoke to every hospital administrator in the city. Time after time, her applications were rejected. "It gets to me every now and then," she admitted to me, "but I'm going to keep on keeping on. All that counts is that first 'yes,' and I've got to believe it will happen." It took several months of steady effort, but it did happen. Today, she's a pediatric nurse in a first-class teaching hospital, and she loves the work.

Both Andy and Maureen had the same basic goal—to get a better job—but one failed, while the other succeeded. What made the critical difference? Andy suffers from a lifelong habit of procrastination. Maureen does not.

Despite Andy's sincere intention to improve his career, he was unable to perform accordingly. He even acted against his own best interests: giving up too soon rather than sticking with the seminars that seemed almost certain to open up new opportunities for him. It was not sheer laziness that sabotaged his dream, nor was it simply a weak will or negative thinking. Instead, it was a firmly entrenched predisposition to procrastinate, featuring its own complicated mixture of self-defeating habits and attitudes. Fortunately, Maureen doesn't have such a chronic predisposition. In pursuing her dream of a better job, she was able to maintain a strong connection between what she wanted to do and what she actually did.

Of course, everybody procrastinates occasionally. An unusually messy closet gets cursed for months without ever being cleaned, or the task of writing an especially difficult letter is put off until the last possible minute. For many people, however, procrastination is chronic, pervasive, and deeply rooted. Because of how, as children, they were conditioned to think, speak, and behave, these individuals have a built-in tendency not only to procrastinate whenever they face a challenging situation but also to do so consistently, in the same way. They don't understand why they do this, and as a result, they're terribly frustrated. So are their family members, friends, and coworkers!

How serious is *your* procrastination problem? To get an idea, ask yourself each of the following questions, circling "YES" if you *often* do what's described, and "NO" if you rarely or never do it:

- Do I put off taking care of important things that jeopardize my relationships, career, finances, or health?   YES   NO

- Do I put off doing what I need to do until a crisis develops?   YES   NO

- Do I put off doing tasks unless I can do them perfectly, or until I can find the perfect time to do them?   YES   NO

- Do I hesitate taking action that needs to be taken because I fear change?   YES   NO

- Do I think too much about things I'd like to do but rarely get around to doing?   YES   NO

- Do I think I am special and don't need to do all the things that other people need to do?   YES   NO

- Do I commit myself to so many things that I can't find time for many of them?   YES   NO

- Do I tend to do only what I *want* to do instead of what I *should* do?   YES   NO

- Do I tend to do only what I think I *should* do instead of what I *want* to do?   YES   NO

If you said yes in response to *any* of these questions, you have a procrastination problem. The more questions to which you answered, the more you will relate to several of the procrastination styles described in this book.

Fortunately, you *can* solve your problem, no matter how long you've suffered from it or how hopelessly trapped you may feel. Reading this book will show you how. First, you'll discover what your own personal patterns of procrastination are. Then you'll learn how you can break these destructive patterns and develop new, more productive ways of thinking, speaking, and acting.

CHRONIC PROCRASTINATORS: THE BIG PICTURE

Although chronic procrastinators have their own idiosyncratic ways of putting things off, they *all* have certain traits and experiences in common. First and foremost, they're filled with good intentions about accomplishing things that are important to them. However, as Will Rogers once said, "Even if you're on the right track, you'll get run over if you just sit there."

Chronic procrastinators wind up sitting too long, and they don't understand why they do this time after time. Despite their good intentions, they feel as if they can't resist avoiding or delaying a challenging task, even when they know that the consequences can hurt them, and even after they've vowed—to themselves and to others—that they won't procrastinate again. Their apparent inability to resist procrastinating causes them to doubt themselves, which results in a lingering sense of powerlessness that all too frequently makes them feel like failures. Some direct this feeling inward and come to regard themselves —at least in certain respects—as worthless, stupid, unreliable, or incompetent. Others direct this feeling outward in the form of anger at the people around them (e.g., "Stop nagging me!" "What's the rush?") or resentment of the situations they're in ("My job stinks!" "I can't take this relationship anymore!").

Second, chronic procrastinators on the whole are also quick to rationalize or excuse their behavior on the grounds that it's nothing they can—or should—do anything about. They'll tell themselves things like "I'm just lazy by nature," or they'll make self-vindicating statements to others, like "Sorry, I'm *always* slow to return phone calls." It's as if their tendency to procrastinate were a fact of life as immutable as natural right-handedness or an allergy to strawberries, rather than an acquired habit capable of being broken. Many times they'll forestall outside criticism by laughing about their procrastination: "You know me," they may joke to a concerned friend, as they finally get around to doing something important. "I put this off as long as I could!" They may even boast about it, as if it were a heroic, daredevil stunt: "I didn't start on this report until last night, and I still got it done by the deadline."

The self-justification that's so commonly practiced by chronic procrastinators is actually a form of self-deception and avoidance. Rather than taking a good look at their problem and learning how to overcome it, they choose to gloss over it, ignoring the pain it has brought them and the difficulties it has created for others.

Third, all chronic procrastinators, at some level, experience recurring regret for not getting things done in a timely manner —a regret that eats away at their capacity to enjoy life and to realize their dreams. Often, procrastinators can literally feel this regret building slowly but surely as the moment of truth draws closer—a frightening feeling that in many cases only reinforces their inertia instead of goading them to act. Thus, the student who regrets not studying for an exam the week before is likely to experience even stronger regret the night before, which can easily cause him or her to sink all the more deeply into a state of paralysis.

This pattern of escalating—and self-paralyzing—regret is particularly apparent among chronic procrastinators who put off filing their income tax returns. Charles, a client of mine several years ago who was an accountant, worked hard taking care of other people's tax returns, but routinely delayed preparing his own. It seems ironic on the surface, but it's actually a typical pattern among chronic procrastinators: not paying attention to their own important personal business. As each tax deadline neared, Charles could sense himself becoming progressively more tense and regretful over avoiding work on his own return, but nevertheless he'd seek out other things to do instead. Ultimately, he failed to file at all for two years in a row, and he's now embroiled in complicated settlement negotiations with the IRS.

Charles's dilemma is far from unique. According to tax attorney Robert S. Fink, author of *How to Defend Yourself Against the IRS* (Simon & Schuster, 1985): "Most people who fail to file tax returns are chronic procrastinators. Greed is not their motive. They don't 'get around' to doing many things in their lives, but when they delay filing income taxes, their procrastination may become a federal crime."

In some cases, when the cost of procrastination is especially high, regret intensifies into guilt or remorse. People can lose their jobs if they're continually late completing projects, and they can lose their relationships if they repeatedly fail to follow through on their commitments. They may even risk their lives. My client Alice, an executive in a fast-growing environmental technology firm, knew for months that she had what she called "a funny spot" in her breast, yet she procrastinated going to the doctor because of fear that something might be "wrong with her." Unfortunately, something *was* wrong. By the time she sought medical care and was diagnosed as having breast cancer, her prognosis was poor—much poorer than it would have been if she had acted more promptly.

Even when procrastination doesn't yield such dire consequences, it inevitably diminishes one's self-esteem, which results in a loss of optimism, happiness, and creative energy. People who suffer from chronic procrastination and do nothing about it find it increasingly difficult to strive toward personal goals or, often, even to formulate them. Ultimately, they may hear themselves saying, "I don't really know who I am" or "I don't really know what I want." When others ask them about their future plans, their reply goes something like this: "I don't know what I'll be doing today, so don't even ask me about tomorrow [or next week, or next year, or five years from now]."

When chronic procrastinators watch a peer or a colleague achieve goals and get ahead while they don't, they worry all the more about their own capabilities. Although they may originally have been just as competent as the person they envy, it's not unusual for them to become *less* competent as time goes by and they continue to procrastinate. By consistently avoiding challenges—or handling them in a rushed, haphazard manner—they may be denying themselves the skill-building experiences they need to sustain and expand their competence.

Rather than *doing* things, many chronic procrastinators tend to spend their time *obsessing* about what they should be doing. Obsessing may feel like thinking, which makes it seem constructive, but it's actually quite different. When procrastinators obsess, their mind is like a dog chasing its tail—they go around and around and around in circles, getting nowhere. Yes, they have a project that needs to be done. Yes, they want to get to it. But no, they just don't do it. Obsessively, they review the reasons why: "I don't feel like doing it now"; "It's too difficult"; "There are too many other things to do." They may also obsess about what will happen if they don't act—failure, humiliation, loss.

But none of their obsessing does any good; indeed, it only makes things worse, increasing the conflicts that are already causing the procrastination. For some, obsessing in this manner can even trigger a serious psychosomatic illness, such as migraine headaches, an ulcer, or colitis—an illness that may provide yet another, much more palpable excuse for failing to act.

The fact that you're reading this book most likely means that you already consider yourself a chronic procrastinator. If so, you probably recognized yourself numerous times in the "big picture" of the chronic procrastinator presented above. But how can you overcome your particular problem? How can you end your personal cycle of disappointed intentions, feeble rationalizations, painful regrets, and diminished self-esteem? How can you stop merely obsessing about your procrastination and, instead, start working to overcome it? The answer lies in the "little picture" —that is, in taking a much closer look than you ever have before at the specific ways in which you procrastinate.

THE SIX STYLES OF PROCRASTINATION

The first step toward positive change is to develop a better understanding of procrastination as a complex *pattern* of living, rather than just a collection of bad habits. Essentially, procrastination is caused by an internal conflict: You feel a want or a need to do something, but you also feel resistant toward doing it. Usually, the two feelings are so evenly matched that you experience a halt in your natural flow of energy until, eventually, the conflict is somehow resolved—often in a way that's not at all satisfying.

In effect, this blockage of energy functions as an approach-avoidance conflict: Like a Hamlet in the world of action, you're torn between two impulses—"to do" or "not to do." Temporarily, at least, you're torn by ambivalence, incapable of making a clear choice or commitment one way or the other. Maybe you actually start doing what you want or need to do, even though your lingering resistance makes you waste a lot of time and energy as you go along. Or maybe you stay stuck in your conflict until the last possible moment, when you finally plunge into doing what you want or need to do (probably with a strong push from someone—or something—else). If so, the task may not get done on time, and if it is, most likely it won't be done nearly as well as it could have been with an earlier start. Or maybe you won't do it at all. You'll stay halted at your sticking point: your flow of energy dammed and, ultimately, damning you to yet another failure.

Far from being lazy, as the stereotype would have it, chronic procrastinators generally have sufficient energy—it just doesn't flow smoothly from mental preparation to physical execution. Instead, it remains mostly mental. Some procrastinators simply can't get beyond the planning stage of a project. They keep elaborating or revising their plans, or generating alternative plans, far beyond the real need to do so. Others preoccupy themselves with wishful thinking: "If only [fill in the blank] happens, I won't have to worry about [fill in the blank]." All get caught up to some degree in the rationalize-regret-and-obsess syndrome we've already observed.

What each chronic procrastinator needs to cultivate is a more natural, more fluid transition from mental activity to physical activity, so that an appropriate amount of time and energy gets allotted to each phase. To do this, the procrastinator first needs to understand the inner conflicts that produced the procrastination pattern. Without that knowledge, the predisposition to procrastinate will sabotage any efforts the individual makes to change, no matter how earnest those efforts may be. It's a situation similar to that faced by many people who try to diet to lose weight without really understanding the inner conflicts that lead them to overeat: Until they learn more about the origins of their eating pattern, their problem will not go away.

I call the sticking point in this kind of internal conflict the
BUT factor, because the chronic procrastinators I've counseled
frequently use the word "but" in describing their action:

"I'd like to finish what I'm doing, *BUT* I want it to be perfect!"
"I'd like to start doing it, *BUT* I hate all those bothersome
    details!"
"I could do it, *BUT* I'm afraid to change!"
"I could do it, *BUT* why should I have to do it?"
"I'd do it now, *BUT* I only get motivated at the last minute!"
"I'd do it now, *BUT* I have so much to do!"

In my thirty years as a psychologist in schools and in private
practice, I have helped hundreds of people from all walks of life
overcome their chronic procrastination. Based upon my experiences as a clinician, I have identified six fundamental procrastination styles, which relate to the six major *BUT* factors:

1. *The Perfectionist: ". . . BUT I want it to be perfect!"*
    Perfectionists can be reluctant to start—or finish—a
task because they don't want to do anything less than a
perfect job. Although their primary concern is not to fall
short of their own lofty standards, they also worry about
failing the high expectations that they believe (rightly or
wrongly) other people have of them. Unfortunately, once
they've begun a task, they often can't resist spending far
more time and energy on it than is required—a commonly
unacknowledged or misunderstood form of procrastination
that involves delaying the completion of a task by *overworking.*
2. *The Dreamer: ". . . BUT I hate all those bothersome details!"*
    The dreamer wants life to be easy and pleasant. Difficult
challenges that confront the dreamer can automatically

provoke resistance: "That might be hard to do" gets translated into "I can't do it." Dreamers are very skillful in developing—and, usually, promoting—grandiose ideas, but they seem incapable of turning their sketchy ideas into full-blown realities: a pattern that frustrates themselves as well as the people around them. Uncomfortable with the practical world, they tend to retreat into fantasies: "Maybe I'll get a lucky break," or "I'm a special person—I don't have to do things the typical [i.e., hardworking] way."

3. *The Worrier: ". . . BUT I'm afraid to change!"*

Worrier procrastinators have an excessive need for security, which causes them to fear risk. They proceed too timidly through life, worrying incessantly about the "what if"s. Faced with a new situation or demand, they become especially anxious, because anything new involves change and, therefore, unknown and potentially undesirable consequences. Thus, they tend to put off making decisions, or following through on decisions, as long as they can. Once they start working on a project, they're likely to drag it out in an effort to help "soften the blow." Many times, consciously or unconsciously, they avoid finishing projects altogether, so that they never have to leave the "comfort zone" of the familiar and move on to new territory. Much to their own dismay and frustration, they resist change even when they know, intellectually, that the change is almost certain to improve their life situation.

4. *The Defier: ". . . BUT why should I have to do it?"*

The defier is a rebel, seeking to buck the rules. Some defiers are openly proud of their tendency to procrastinate, precisely because it goes against the "normal" or "logical" way to do things. By procrastinating, they are setting their own schedule—one that nobody else can predict or control. In other words, they are establishing their individuality, against the expectations of others. Other defiers are more subtle, perhaps because they are less consciously aware of what they are doing. They don't flaunt their opposition toward doing something. They simply don't take on the responsibility to do it in a timely manner. This more subtle type of defiance is called "passive-aggressive" behavior. Both kinds of defier procrastinators are inclined to see relatively simple tasks—like doing the laundry, paying the bills, or maintaining a car—as big impositions on their time and energy, rather than as things they should take in stride as mature adults.

5. *The Crisis-Maker: ". . . BUT I only get motivated at the last minute!"*

The crisis-maker needs to live on the edge. Addicted to the adrenaline rush of intense emotion, constant challenge, and emergency action, crisis-makers delight in pulling things off at the last minute. To them, procrastination is a form of adventure. Adventures, however, are by nature risky, and the crisis-maker procrastinator is often a loser. Despite the heroic, last-minute run, the train is missed. Despite working day and night all weekend, the status report doesn't get completed by Monday. Despite a year-long intention to spend July in Europe, the flight isn't booked on time and the deadline for a reduced fare passes quietly by, too quietly for the crisis-maker to notice.

6. *The Overdoer: ". . . BUT I have so much to do!"*

Overdoer procrastinators say "yes" to too much because they are unable—or unwilling—to make choices and establish priorities. In other words, they haven't really mastered the art of decision-making. Because of this liability, they tend to be inefficient in managing time, organizing resources, and resolving conflicts. The result is that they try to do too much at once and, inevitably, fail. Overdoers are often hard workers, and many of them do accomplish some things very well; however, other things never get done at all, or else get done poorly or late. With so much to do and so little time to do it in, overdoers are prime candidates for early burnout.

Each of these six procrastination styles—the perfectionist, the dreamer, the worrier, the defier, the crisis-maker, and the over-doer—involves a distinctly different pattern of impeding the productive flow of energy. But rarely does a flesh-and-blood procrastinator display only *one* of these styles. Instead, each person employs a distinctive *mix* of styles: perhaps two or three styles that are the most operative—the major styles—along with two or three that are displayed less often but are still reasonably active—the minor styles.

For example, a person initially identified as a perfectionist procrastinator may also have a dreamer inside, who, among other activities, delights in imagining "perfect" life situations. As a result, sometimes the person's procrastination style is recognizably that of a perfectionist; other times, that of a dreamer. Within this same person, there may also be a bit of the crisis-maker, who performs best under pressure.

In fact, chronic procrastinators tend to harbor several—or even all—of the six procrastination styles to some degree, with different kinds of life situations triggering different kinds of styles. For example, a woman may identify herself as primarily a crisis-maker procrastinator—especially at work, where she has plenty of opportunities to find, or engineer, emergency situations. Nevertheless, with a little more self-analysis, she may realize that she procrastinates somewhat differently in other areas of her life. When it comes to fulfilling her innermost desires, she may function more like a dreamer procrastinator. And with her husband, the strongest relationship in her life, she may adopt a defier style.

Self-assessment quizzes at the end of this chapter will enable you to identify your personal repertoire of procrastination styles. The following six chapters explore in depth each of the six major procrastination styles. These chapters will guide you in understanding the origins and functions of your procrastination styles, and tell you how you can replace them with more effective ways of thinking, speaking, and acting. The final chapter provides a wealth of motivational ideas for continuing on the road toward change, so that you can begin living more consciously, happily, and productively than you ever have before.

THE LEARNING AND UNLEARNING PROCESS

It's hardly surprising that chronic procrastinators tend to put off dealing with—or even acknowledging—their dilemma. Many resort instinctively to denial ("It's no big deal!"), projection ("It's not my problem—it's someone [everyone] else's!"), or rationalization ("There are lots of good reasons why I'm sometimes behind schedule."). They cling to the knowledge that deep down they mean well—the "good intentions" part of the procrastination syndrome that I discussed earlier—and therefore that no "deep-down" self-examination is necessary. They couldn't be more wrong!

To appreciate the truly insidious nature and extent of your own inclination to procrastinate, and to realize how intricately embedded into your thoughts and deeds this inclination is, you need take a good, hard look at your life and the family in which you grew up. You were not *born* a procrastinator; you had to *learn* to procrastinate. Your major education in thinking, speaking, and acting took place during childhood, and your major teachers were your parents and early caretakers.

John, a thirty-six-year-old social studies teacher, came to my office complaining about his "lack of self-worth," but it soon became apparent that his more pressing problem was chronic procrastination. Formerly a professional pianist, he had played in jazz clubs and concert halls throughout the metropolitan New York area. He loved this work, but after marrying, he reluctantly gave it up and became a high school teacher in order to have a more stable income. Eventually, he stopped playing the piano altogether—even at home. Ever afterward, he kept meaning to start playing again, *BUT* he never seemed able to find the "right" time to do so.

As John and I explored his family dynamics during childhood, he came to appreciate what a strong influence his father had been on his thinking, his speaking, and his behavior. His father was always praising people who did things better than anyone else, and putting down those who were "second best." John learned to do the same. He incorporated into his belief system his father's opinion that a person must do things perfectly or not at all. Now, whenever John had a notion to start playing the piano again, he would stop himself by thinking: ". . . *BUT* I'll be rusty!" Naturally, he *would* be rusty, yet why should that stop him? It stopped him because, for that deep-down part of John that was still obedient and wanted to please his father, "rusty" was totally unacceptable.

Just thinking about playing the piano made John exaggerate his ineptness so that he would conjure up images of being ridiculed by others for even trying to play. These images had no basis in reality, but they did serve to raise his anxiety and reinforce his procrastination. The *BUT* factor that fueled his procrastination was: " . . . *BUT* I must be perfect!" In other words, he was a perfectionist procrastinator; and he was first set on that

torturous path—with all good intentions—by another perfectionist, his father. In order to overcome his procrastination, John
needed to learn specific ways of thinking, speaking, and acting
that would counteract his childhood programming. Some of these
ways are discussed in Chapter 2.

A different example of early family influences molding a
chronic procrastinator was presented to me by my client Alison,
a forty-nine-year-old executive secretary. For years, she had
yearned to quit her job, move to California, and begin a new life.
Her husband was willing to join her in the move, but she just
couldn't commit to it. She told me that before she could let
herself risk it, she needed a "strong guarantee" that the move
was the right thing to do.

When Alison and I discussed her childhood, she told me how
difficult life had been for her mother and father, growing up
during the Great Depression of the 1930s. When they became
parents, they were continually worried and pessimistic, fearing
that tragedy always lurked right around the corner. Alison found
her parents' fear contagious: Throughout childhood and on into
adulthood, she repeatedly paralyzed herself with nervousness. In
her mind, she would go over and over the dreadful possibilities
that might lie in the future: "What if I do join the game, *BUT*
the other kids don't like me?" "What if I do study hard today,
BUT I just can't think of the answer when the teacher calls on
me tomorrow?" "What if I do move to California, *BUT* I can't
find a job?"

Instead of getting beyond these *BUT*s, Alison would let them
stop her or slow her down to the point where she felt safer,
though, ultimately, still frustrated. As a child, she'd wait so long
to make a decision about joining the game that, finally, it would
be too late to join. She'd put off studying until the last minute
and, as a result, suffer even greater anxiety about the teacher's
calling on her. And now she was delaying her move to Califor-

nia—thereby ensuring, ironically, her continued involvement in a New York job that she detested! Clearly, a major *BUT* factor for Alison, as for her parents, was fear: ". . . *BUT* I'm afraid!" And so Alison grew up to be a worrier procrastinator. Like John the perfectionist, Alison the worrier had to learn new ways of thinking, speaking, and, acting that would supersede her childhood training to procrastinate. Some of these ways are discussed in Chapter 4.

At the end of this chapter, you will be invited to perform six self-assessment quizzes, based on your current ways of thinking, speaking, and acting. These quizzes will help you determine your personal *BUT* factors and procrastination styles, both major and minor. In addition to completing these quizzes as honestly as you can, you will need to scrutinize your childhood to gain a better appreciation of how the childhood messages you received contributed to the kind of chronic procrastinator you are. Start now by asking yourself the following questions—questions you can continue to ponder as you read through this book:

How did my parents (or early caretakers) respond to major challenges they faced? What might I have learned from this?

What messages did my parents communicate to me—by words or deeds—regarding:
- spending time, wasting time?
- taking a risk, staying safe?
- the importance of work, the importance of play?
- the need to be responsible, the consequences of irresponsibility?
- what constitutes "success," and what constitutes "failure"?
- my own personal competencies and incompetencies?

What impact did each of these messages have on me?

What's my own viewpoint on these issues now?

Always bear in mind that you don't have to remain at the mercy of those early unfortunate teachings that led you to procrastinate. Once you understand them more clearly, you can face them and say, "No, I'm not going to let them rule my life anymore."

Also, be sure to consider each of the three different ways in which you learned to procrastinate: the ways that you *think*, the ways that you *speak*, and the ways that you *act*. In the popular imagination, procrastination is too often associated only with a person's behavior—whether he or she delays starting something, or drags out doing it, or fails to complete it on time, or does it at all. Equally important and consequential, however, is what's going on in a person's mind (thoughts, attitudes, and emotions) and what comes out of a person's mouth (exclamations, dialogue, and "self-talk").

For example, a man in the advertising business may come to realize that he consistently procrastinates working on projects for one of his long-term clients by waiting until the last minute to get started. This discovery is a useful "first step" in his effort to overcome his personal procrastination problem; but it can be even more helpful for him to investigate the thinking or speaking habits that may lie behind—and motivate—his behavior:

What are his *thoughts* relating to the client? Maybe he feels especially intimidated by this person. Maybe the client reminds him of an overly demanding teacher in his past.

What are his *thoughts* relating to the work? Maybe he has always resented performing exactly this kind of work—at home, in school, and now on the job.

How does he *speak* about this client—or any other person like this client? Maybe he tends to ridicule such an individual to his colleagues.

How does he *speak* about the work he performs for his client? Maybe he finds himself saying things like "This work is so demeaning, I'll get to it when I'm good and ready!"

Each of these habits of thinking and speaking offers a clue that he may be a "defier" procrastinator—something he may not fully comprehend if he considers only his actions.

To change from a procrastinator to a non-procrastinator, you need to follow a similar, three-part approach: working to change your negative *thinking* and *speaking* patterns as well as your negative *acting* patterns. That is why, in discussing each of the six procrastination styles in the chapters that follow, I provide a detailed three-part program for change, which includes specific recommendations for positive thinking, speaking, and acting. This program will help you change your *BUT* factors (opposition and blockage) into *AND* factors (connection and resolution), as in the following model:

The BUT Path	*The AND Path*
. . . *BUT* I don't want to do this!	. . . *AND* I will get it done!
. . . *BUT* it's so difficult!	. . . *AND* I'll give it the time and energy it needs!
. . . *BUT* I want to watch TV!	. . . *AND* I'll work now and watch TV later!

... *BUT* I want it to be perfect!   ... *AND* I'll complete it on
                                    time even if every little de-
                                    tail is not quite perfect.

Other books and programs on procrastination make the mistake of arguing that overcoming procrastination is simply a matter of "getting better organized" or "managing time more
effectively." In actuality, the syndrome of procrastination is
much more complicated than that, necessitating more specific
practical and personal guidance.

The chapters that follow, which focus separately on each of
the six procrastination styles, also discuss more specifically how
family dynamics can cause a child to develop a particular style.
As you read these discussions, ponder your own childhood, paying special attention to any memories that are similar in content,
spirit, or effect to those described. The more you engage in this
kind of close introspection, the more images will arise to reveal
clues about how you first learned to procrastinate. This knowledge is valuable, for it can make the work of "unlearning" your
procrastination patterns better targeted and easier to accomplish.

This book will help you develop a more natural flow of time
and energy in your life, which works *for* you, not against you,
which *builds,* not weakens, your self-esteem. You will not be
asked to be somebody else, who is more efficient, or to do things
somebody else's way: the presumptively "right" way. Instead,
this book assists you to realize and live the way that you know
deep inside is right for *you.* It invites you to change from your
personal path of avoidance—the *BUT* path—to your personal
path of resolution—the *AND* path.

DISCOVERING MY PROCRASTINATION STYLES: SIX SELF-ASSESSMENT QUIZZES

Directions:

1. Complete each of the six quizzes as follows:

   After considering each question as honestly as you can, circle the answer that best reflects your own experience:
   F = frequently
   S = sometimes
   R = rarely or never

   After completing all the questions in a single quiz, count the circled "F"s, multiply this number by 2, and enter the total in the space marked SUBTOTAL "F" × 2.

   Count the circled "S"s and enter this total in the space marked SUBTOTAL "S."

   Add the two SUBTOTALS and enter the total in the space marked TOTAL SCORE.

2. After completing all six quizzes, complete the section entitled MY MAJOR AND MINOR STYLES as follows:

   In the column marked "Total Score," enter the total score for each quiz in the appropriate space.

   In the column marked "Major," enter a check mark next to any style for which your total score is 10 or above. This identifies a major procrastination style.

In the column marked "Minor," enter a check mark next to any style for which your total score is 9 or less. This identifies a minor procrastination style.

In the column marked "Rank," enter the appropriate rank for each style, as follows: 1 = highest total score, 2 = next-highest total score, and so on, through 6. If two or more styles have the same total scores, give them the same rank.

NOTE: To gain a better overall understanding of procrastination, read *all* the chapters that follow. However, pay particularly close attention to those chapters covering the procrastination styles that most affect you, according to your self-assessment results: *all major styles* and *all minor styles with total scores over 5.* The higher you ranked an individual style, the more attention you should give it.

1. Perfectionist Procrastinator: Quiz

(Circle one: F = frequently; S = sometimes; R = rarely or never)

(*a*) Do I get preoccupied with details, rules, or schedules that others don't seem to care much about?   F   S   R

(*b*) Do I have difficulty starting or completing a project because my own standards haven't been met?   F   S   R

(*c*) Am I reluctant to delegate tasks or work with others unless they do things my way?   F   S   R

(*d*) Do others comment on my being rigid, stubborn, or finicky?   F   S   R

(*e*) Am I critical of what I've accomplished or how long it took me to do it?   F   S   R

(*f*) Am I satisfied with what I do only if it is as good as it can possibly be?   F   S   R

(*g*) Do I look at my failures as embarrassments that I would hate to mention or have revealed?   F   S   R

(*h*) Do I have difficulty maintaining a sense of humor while I'm struggling to do something new?   F   S   R

(*i*) Do I feel upset or humiliated if I don't do something as well as one of my peers?   F   S   R

(*j*) Do I think about situations in extremes— black or white, ignoring the gray area in between?   F   S   R

SUBTOTAL "F" × 2 = _____

SUBTOTAL "S" = _____

TOTAL SCORE (add SUBTOTALS) = _____

2. Dreamer Procrastinator: Quiz

(Circle one: F = frequently; S = sometimes; R = rarely or never)

(a) Do I think a lot about what I'd like to accomplish but rarely get projects off the ground?   F   S   R

(b) Do I wait for opportunities to drop into my lap rather than take an active, "go get 'em" approach?   F   S   R

(c) No matter how old I am, do I still wonder what I'm going to be or do "when I grow up"?   F   S   R

(d) Do I spend more time thinking about the finished project than about the details needed to get it done?   F   S   R

(e) Do I long to be able to go from "A" to "Z" without having to deal with the stuff in between?   F   S   R

(f) Do I wish someone else would handle the bothersome details of life, freeing me to do what's creative?   F   S   R

(g) Do I find myself thinking or speaking words like "One of these days, I will . . ."?   F   S   R

(h) Do other people sometimes accuse me of being a dreamer, of having my head in the clouds?   F   S   R

(i) Do I do what I feel like at the moment, forgetting or ignoring previous plans or priorities?   F   S   R

(j) Do I expect great things from myself but wonder why they never seem to happen?   F   S   R

SUBTOTAL "F" × 2 = _____

SUBTOTAL "S" = _____

TOTAL SCORE (add SUBTOTALS) = _____

3. Worrier Procrastinator: Quiz
(Circle one: F = frequently, S = sometimes; R = rarely or never)

(*a*) Do I have difficulty making decisions, vacil-
lating about what I *should* do?   F   S   R

(*b*) Do I need—or seek—approval, advice, or as-
surance from others before I do things?   F   S   R

(*c*) Do I have trouble starting projects or working
on my own because I doubt my judgment or
ability?   F   S   R

(*d*) Do I think things are too much for me, or
worry about overdoing it?   F   S   R

(*e*) Do I hesitate to leave my "comfort zone,"
avoiding situations that might cause stress or
anxiety?   F   S   R

(*f*) Do I become easily fatigued or agitated when
something disrupts my normal routine?   F   S   R

(*g*) Do I have difficulty initiating conversations or
speaking up for myself?   F   S   R

(*h*) Do I sometimes paralyze myself before starting
work on a project, wondering about the "what
if's"?   F   S   R

(*i*) Do I exaggerate the trouble that might arise
from a situation, or minimize my ability to
cope with it?   F   S   R

(*j*) Do I think I could do more—or better—if
somebody would take me by the hand and
show me the way?   F   S   R

SUBTOTAL "F" × 2 = _____

SUBTOTAL "S" = _____

TOTAL SCORE (add SUBTOTALS) = _____

4. Defier Procrastinator: Quiz

(Circle one: F = frequently; S = sometimes; R = rarely or never)

(*a*) Do I become sulky, irritable, or argumentative
when asked to do something I don't want to
do?   F   S   R

(*b*) Do I work deliberately slowly or ineffectively
in order to sabotage a task I don't like doing?   F   S   R

(*c*) Do I feel resentful or manipulated when I
wind up having to do something unex-
pectedly?   F   S   R

(*d*) Do I feel that others make unreasonable demands on me?   F   S   R

(*e*) Do I avoid obligations by claiming that I've
forgotten them or that they're not important?   F   S   R

(*f*) When people ask me why I did or didn't do
something, do I feel they are hassling me?   F   S   R

(*g*) Do I believe that I'm doing a better job than
others think—or say—I'm doing?   F   S   R

(*h*) Do I take offense at suggestions from others
regarding how I could be more productive?   F   S   R

(*i*) Do others accuse me of—or get annoyed with
me for—failing to do my share of work effi-
ciently?   F   S   R

(*j*) Do I frequently criticize or ridicule people
who are in authority?   F   S   R

SUBTOTAL "F" × 2 = _____

SUBTOTAL "S" = _____

TOTAL SCORE (add SUBTOTALS) = _____

5. Crisis-Maker Procrastinator: Quiz
(Circle one: F = frequently; S = sometimes; R = rarely or never)

(a) Do I ignore important tasks, then, at the last
minute, work frantically to get them done?   F   S   R

(b) Do I feel that life is chaotic and that I can
never be sure what the next day will bring?   F   S   R

(c) Do my moods change rapidly and dramatically?   F   S   R

(d) Do I get easily frustrated and show it by dis-
playing anger or quitting?   F   S   R

(e) Do I act in ways that other people find pro-
vocative, seductive, or attention-getting?   F   S   R

(f) Am I easily influenced by circumstances, responding to the need of the moment?   F   S   R

(g) Do I enjoy—or pride myself on—taking risks
or living on the edge?   F   S   R

(h) Do I temporarily get very involved with someone or something, then abruptly detach myself
and move on?   F   S   R

(i) Do I think of my life as so dramatic that it
could be made into a soap opera?   F   S   R

(j) Do I prefer action, having little patience for
things that are too slow, predictable, or safe?   F   S   R

SUBTOTAL "F" × 2 = _____

SUBTOTAL "S" = _____

TOTAL SCORE (add SUBTOTALS) = _____

6. Overdoer Procrastinator: Quiz

(Circle one: F = frequently; S = sometimes; R = rarely or never)

(a) Do I run around doing things, without really feeling that I'm accomplishing very much?   F   S   R

(b) Do I have difficulty saying "no" to people who ask for help, then feel resentful later?   F   S   R

(c) When I'm doing a task, do I wonder, "How did I get myself into this?"   F   S   R

(d) Do I give priority to what I think I *should* do, putting off what I really *want* to do?   F   S   R

(e) Do I find myself complaining, "I have no time," "I have too much to do," or "I'm too busy"?   F   S   R

(f) Do I find new things to do instead of catching up with things when I get unexpected free time?   F   S   R

(g) Does my attention easily get diverted from what I'm doing to something else?   F   S   R

(h) Do I get overinvolved in other people's problems, postponing attention to my own?   F   S   R

(i) Do other people talk about—or regard—me as someone who will drop everything if and when they need me?   F   S   R

(j) Do I enjoy being busy, but secretly think that maybe I don't know how to be any other way?   F   S   R

SUBTOTAL "F" × 2 = _____

SUBTOTAL "S" = _____

TOTAL SCORE (add SUBTOTALS) = _____

MY MAJOR AND MINOR STYLES

Style	*Total Score*	*Major* (10 or more)	*Minor* (9 or less)	*Rank* (1 = highest)
1. Perfectionist	_____	_____	_____	_____
2. Dreamer	_____	_____	_____	_____
3. Worrier	_____	_____	_____	_____
4. Defier	_____	_____	_____	_____
5. Crisis-Maker	_____	_____	_____	_____
6. Overdoer	_____	_____	_____	_____

Chapter 2

The Perfectionist Procrastinator

". . . <u>But</u> I want it to be perfect!"

What's wrong with trying to be perfect? In the abstract, "perfectionism" certainly seems like a virtue. Although we may occasionally poke fun at individual perfectionists—calling them fusspots, nitpickers, or grinds—we tend to admire the sheer loftiness of their ambition. Shouldn't we *all* try to achieve the highest possible standards in everything we do? Isn't the noblest, most laudable, and most rewarding endeavor in life to strive for the best?

The sad reality is that having perfection as a goal is a much more complicated matter than aiming for excellence or for a high level of achievement. In many cases, a preoccupation with perfection can actually sabotage one's own best efforts. It then becomes a curse, breeding a special kind of procrastination that frustrates not only the perfectionists themselves but also their family members, friends, and associates. Consider the following two examples: Robert and David.

Robert, a thirty-eight-year-old accountant who owns his own firm, is an open and avowed perfectionist. He freely admits that he is a compulsive worker and that everything he does must be flawless, and his devotion to this goal is obvious to those around him. He works long, hard hours at the office, brings work home most nights and weekends, and always looks concerned, preoccupied, and overburdened.

Because Robert is always working, he doesn't seem to be a procrastinator as well as a perfectionist, but in fact he is. He seldom finishes a project unless—or until—there's a pressing deadline. Instead, he repeatedly finds one more thing to do in order to make the project better. And he puts off doing anything that doesn't relate directly to his work. He hasn't taken a real vacation in five years, despite his wife's pleading, and he rarely gets around to helping his daughter with her school studies, reading one of the novels he's bought, or completing a task on the family's ever-growing list of home repairs.

Robert feels most comfortable working within the strategic, detail-oriented world of the office that he himself controls, not in the world of his home, where he must collaborate with frustrating non-perfectionists or engage in activities that are new, different, or difficult. But even doing office work, he has a nagging feeling that things are not right. He wonders why he can't "get away" with working a forty-hour week and why he can't break personal habits that are clearly detrimental to himself and his family.

David, a forty-four-year-old physician who displays a fun-loving, easygoing personality, has a different way of procrastinating. He waits until the last minute to start working on a task, then he rushes through it.

Last year, David committed himself six months in advance to giving a lecture at a major professional conference. One week before the event, a friend, who also planned to attend, asked if David wanted any help with his speech. The friend was flabbergasted when David blithely answered, "I haven't begun to write it yet." At the conference, David did manage to make an acceptable—although unremarkable—presentation. His friend was once again startled when David remarked, "Of course, if only I'd had more time, I would have done a much better job."

On the surface, David appears to take a casual, even flippant, approach to things. Other people don't suspect the turmoil and discontent that lie beneath this carefully cultivated facade. The goals he creates for himself are so unrealistically high that they paralyze him from going forward. To protect his self-esteem, he "handicaps" the situation by starting late, so that he has a built-in excuse for not meeting his own intimidating standards. And to protect his image with others, he doesn't let them see how much he cares and how demanding he is toward himself.

Often, David procrastinates simply to buy himself relief from the burden of thinking he has to be perfect. Unfortunately, he pays a high price for that relief. If he doesn't call himself sufficiently to account *before* a deadline, he's twice as hard on himself afterward. He's an excellent Monday-morning quarterback, analyzing what he did wrong, what he should have done instead, and how stupid he was for not doing things the self-proclaimed "right way." Now, when he recalls his presentation at the conference, he privately agonizes over the great opportunity he blew by waiting so long to prepare. "Why do I always do things this way?" he wonders.

Robert and David are both moderately successful men, but they are all too keenly aware that something's wrong in the way they function. They know that despite their best efforts or intentions, they are not as happy or fulfilled as they would like to be. They realize that somehow they are sabotaging their own lives, limiting their capacity to achieve, to grow, and to enjoy.

Robert and David may be opposites in certain respects—Robert the hardworking sourpuss vs. David the easygoing charmer —but there's one significant, self-defeating attribute they share: Both are "perfectionist procrastinators." No matter what guise they may present to the outside world, perfectionist procrastinators all share these three, interrelated characteristics:

1. *Because perfectionist procrastinators are idealists, they can be very unrealistic in their use of time and energy.*

Perfectionists are extreme in their thinking: If they're

going to do something, they reason, they should do the best possible job that can be done. There's no acceptable "middle ground." Since few real-life situations can be defined in terms of a "perfect" outcome, this type of thinking usually leads to performance standards based on personal fantasies of perfection, not on the practicalities of the situation at hand. Faced with a demand task, perfectionists are inevitably torn between two extremes: giving it all they've got, or giving it up altogether. Robert strives to do the former in his office work—at the expense of his home life—while David comes as close as he dares to doing the latter.

In contrast to perfectionists, high achievers strive for *excellence* rather than *perfection* in what they do. They define their goals—and evaluate their performance in meeting their goals—far more realistically, allowing more freedom to act and broader criteria for determining "successful" accomplishment.

High-achieving athletes, for example, will set reasonable, season-by-season standards for themselves that are aimed at helping them realize their "personal best," not some superhuman vision of perfection. Similarly, they won't put off training on a given day because they suspect they might not perform "perfectly." Instead, they will do their personal best in the context of each day that goes by.

Perfectionists, unlike high achievers, don't think, "I want to do the best *that I can do now*," but rather, "I want to do the best *that can possibly be done*." The real-life "I" and the real-life circumstances get sacrificed to an elusive, ultimately impossible ideal.

2. *Fearing failure so much, perfectionist procrastinators tend to put off starting tasks or delay their completion.*

Perfectionists know that they run an extremely high risk of failing to meet their goal of perfection, and this breeds a corresponding high degree of anxiety. For them, failing at a task does not mean simply that the task was not performed successfully; instead, it represents a personal indictment. Because they stake their self-esteem so entirely on being perfect, failure indicates that they are inadequate, worthless, even shameful or guilty. It's small wonder, then, that perfectionists seek to avoid failure at all costs.

Some perfectionists (like Robert) seek to prevent failure by "overworking" tasks, in a compulsive effort to add as many praiseworthy touches as possible and to eliminate any possible grounds for criticism. They feel they must have complete control over every detail of the task, to avoid the risk of intolerable "imperfections." The frequent result is that the task doesn't get done—or is finished at the very last moment, which is often much later than the original deadline.

Other perfectionists (like David) seek to forestall failure by using procrastination as a defense. Their shaky logic goes as follows: If they choose not to take a particular challenge seriously—either by not doing anything at all about it or by treating it in a very offhand, casual manner—they can spare themselves the tyrannical, self-imposed responsibility to be perfect. If they can create a situation in which circumstances are "beyond their control," they can have an excuse for not achieving perfection.

Hence, David allows himself so little time to write his speech that he can't expect himself do a perfect job. Procrastination, he believes, is a better alternative than the unthinkable: using the full amount of available time and then failing or feeling unsatisfied. And when he feels pressured to "save face" with a friend—a pressure he imposes on himself—he misleadingly implies that he would have done better if only he'd had more time.

A perfectionist's fear of failure can cause him or her to

dread *any* change in the status quo that presents new challenges—ironically, even the prospect of success. Behind David's hesitancy to take full advantage of professional opportunities is his fear that he might not be able to live up to the image—or the demands—that a more successful career would impose upon him. As Irving Berlin once said, "The toughest thing about being a success is that you have to keep on being a success." And after each major achievement, people develop a higher standard for future success.

For a perfectionist like David, success may stir up unusually profound feelings of insecurity, self-doubt, and self-criticism—feelings he may express to himself in the following ways: "Will I be able to live up to the expectations that others now have of me?" "Did I genuinely succeed, or was I merely lucky?" "Does my new success truly reflect the best that I can do, or could I possibly have done even better?"

3. *Perfectionist procrastinators tend to see everything in life as a burden, making it much more difficult for them to do individual tasks in a timely manner.*

Because their standards and expectations are so high, perfectionists are inclined to derive less satisfaction from day-to-day life than their non-perfectionist counterparts. Instead of being able to relax and have fun with tasks—or at least take them in stride—they are constantly making them burdensome and difficult, focusing on how far short of perfection things fall, and all that could, should, or must be done in order to make up the difference. What's more, they continue to mull over past lapses from perfection and to worry about future demands for perfection. Like Robert, they may wind up perpetually concerned, preoccupied, and overwhelmed—which is a poor state of mind for living happily in the present. Or like David, they may develop into chronic avoiders or bogglers—acting *against* time instead of learning to work *with* time more productively.

Perfectionists also suffer other forms of general "life oppression" that adversely affect their ability to function in an efficient and effective manner. They have difficulty congratulating themselves, accepting compliments from others, or even making progress toward self-improvement, because their inner voice of self-criticism is so loud and incessant. Like Robert, they take little energy-recharging pleasure from their accomplishments; and like David, they can't stop kicking themselves for their mistakes long enough to devise a practical plan for doing better.

What's more, perfectionists are inclined to turn potential allies into adversaries. They resist allowing other people to help them with burdensome tasks because of their perfection-driven need to exercise as much control over those tasks as possible, not to mention their need to appear self-sufficient. Thus Robert, the owner of his company, becomes a "doer," rather than the "manager" he should be, by refusing to delegate part of his huge workload; and thus David cuts himself off from any outside help on his speech— even though his speech might have benefited greatly from it.

Finally, in addition to being self-critical, perfectionists often become critical of others for their "slipshod" way of doing things—which is why Robert finds it difficult to perform tasks at home with his wife and daughter. Perfectionists may even feel compelled to correct inconsequential "mistakes" that another person makes rather than simply let them be. This impulse toward extraneous critical activity only consumes more of the perfectionist's day-to-day time and energy.

To gain a greater understanding of how these three basic characteristics interrelate in the life of a perfectionist procrastinator, let's take an extensive look at another case study from my practice. The study will also give us some valuable insights into how this syndrome develops and, even more importantly, how it can ultimately be overcome.

KAREN: THE PERFECTIONIST PROCRASTINATOR

When Karen became my client, she was a thirty-nine-year-old public relations manager, a part-time graduate student, and a wife in her twelfth year of marriage. The first time she walked into my office, I was struck by how extraordinarily well groomed she was. She wore expensive wool slacks and a fashionable sweater, with attractive accessories to match. Her short, dark hair was stylish and meticulously combed, as if she had just come from a session at a hair salon. Her fingernails were elegantly manicured, and her makeup was flawless. Yet despite her polished, carefully composed appearance, I could sense that she was ill at ease and didn't know how to begin.

"Tell me what brought you here," I asked.

Karen struggled for words. "It's all gotten too much for me—my whole life," she stated, shaking her head. "I thought I had it together; but lately I feel as though I'm falling apart." Tears welled up in her eyes, although she was doing her utmost to ignore them.

Finally, the words came spilling out: "Why does everything I do have to be such an ordeal? There's never a moment when I'm not wound up. When I do something wrong, I can't stop being mad at myself. And if other people screw up, or don't do things the way I think they should, it drives me crazy. I can't figure out why I get so worked up over little things that don't really matter, that other people don't seem to notice or care about. Or why it takes me forever to get things done. Like this morning— I spent over an hour getting dressed to go out, and even then I felt rushed. I couldn't seem to get anything right!"

As Karen continued to pour out her frustrations, it became clear to me that she was a perfectionist. She felt compelled to meet the highest possible standards in everything she did. But having neither the time nor the energy to accomplish all her goals, she was constantly on edge. The only way she'd found to relieve some of the pressure caused by her compulsive need for perfection was to procrastinate. Over the next few months, we explored the different ways that procrastination affected each major aspect of her existence: her work, her graduate studies, her marriage, and her goal of self-fulfillment.

Procrastinating at Work

At first, Karen derived a lot of excitement from her job as a manager at a young, fast-growing public relations firm. She thought of it as an ideal job that would eventually bring her total fulfillment. She loved working at full tilt, there was plenty of work to do, and she did it very well.

It took only a small number of mistakes, a couple of minor setbacks, and—perhaps most devastating of all—a few words of criticism for Karen's initial enthusiasm to evaporate. As a per- fectionist, she simply could not accept these "imperfect" devel- opments, and so she committed herself to a work pattern that she thought would allow the greatest possibility for the type of high-level success she wanted: She would either work 100 per- cent on something, or else let it go until she could. Regrettably, this pattern proved ineffective, wasting a great deal of her time and causing her many other difficulties as well.

Karen was well aware of some of the problems she was creating for herself. For example, she overprepared for every presentation to a client or a colleague, regardless of its level of importance to the business. Also, because she was so concerned about not being able to say "just the right thing" on the telephone, she would put off returning phone calls and would fax or post a letter instead: something that took much more time for her to do and much more time to yield a response.

Other self-made problems plaguing Karen were so multifaceted and so ingrained in her day-to-day work habits that she began to appreciate them only after several months of therapy. For example, almost every time she felt that she was near to completing a task at work, she would begin tearing it apart. She would hunt for things that were wrong and then exaggerate their impact. Reviewing a subordinate's almost finished press release, for instance, Karen would say to herself something like, "This press release is awful! The word 'fabulous' is used twice. We can't send it out." Thus, thanks to Karen's perfectionism, a simple word repetition, easily correctable, would render the entire release unacceptable. She would make matters worse by misusing her own valuable time to redo the release from scratch. Because of the delay, the release would wind up being issued later than originally scheduled, resulting in less press coverage.

In general, Karen had trouble setting practical and reasonable time limits for her projects at work. Instead of creating time-related milestones for various stages of a task, she took the attitude that everything remained, in her words, "undone and redoable" until the last conceivable moment, which was usually the ultimate deadline imposed upon her by the company.

For example, there was a time when Karen had a month to put together a progress report for her boss on one of her long-term projects. As the days went by, she found herself totally bogged down in writing version after version of it. A few days before it was due, she had accumulated four different "rough" versions of the report—none of which satisfied her. In other words, she had spent roughly 400 percent more of her time and energy than was appropriate. Understandably, she felt stressed out. She complained of being *overworked;* but in fact, she was *overworking.* It was not a case of too much work to do in too little time but, rather, too much time doing too much work.

Karen frequently missed important deadlines. Sometimes it was because she couldn't stop working on a project. She felt either that she hadn't done all that she should do or that it wasn't as good as it could be. Other times, it was because she avoided working on the project due to her anxiety about it. If a project seemed too difficult to handle, she would seek every excuse she could find, every diversion she could create, to get away from it. Telling herself that she was gearing up to work on a project, she might spend an entire hour unnecessarily organizing and reorganizing work papers. Finally, she might begin working on it, only to stop midstream and switch to something else. She often used other people's needs as an escape from her own work— sometimes actively looking for imperfections in their work that she could correct.

Because of these habits, Karen always had dozens of unfinished projects on her desk or on her mind. To a superficial observer, it might have appeared that she was simply a very busy worker, or that she was just a disorganized or easily distracted person. In fact, she was only behaving like a classic perfectionist procrastinator.

Procrastinating in School

Karen's career as a part-time graduate student promised to be an indefinitely long and arduous one—not because she lacked intelligence (she was quite smart), and not because she wasn't dedicated (she signed up for two courses each and every semester), but because here, too, her perfectionism drove her to procrastinate. Since she put off certain particularly onerous assignments until the last minute or spent more time and energy on others than was necessary, Karen often requested an "incomplete" grade near the end of the term rather than accept anything less than an "A." This ploy meant that she had to carry over extra work from one semester to the next, making her schoolwork progressively more difficult.

I asked Karen, "What does 'less than an "A"' mean to you? What if you did get a 'B'?" I could see the discomfort my question provoked. She squirmed in her chair, uncrossed her legs, patted her hair, recrossed her legs, and looked around the room, as if the answer might be hiding somewhere.

"I know it's silly," she finally responded, sounding like a little girl, "but for me, an 'A' means doing what I should have done. But a 'B' . . . that means I've been judged as inadequate, that I'm not as good as the 'A' students. In my own opinion, I've failed."

"What about an 'incomplete'?" I countered. "What does *that* mean to you?"

This time, Karen's response was immediate and assured: "An 'incomplete' means I could still get an 'A,' if I really try hard enough. There are times when I wonder if I'm only conning myself, but deep down, I truly believe that if I have enough time to work on a paper or a test, I'll do a super job. It's not a matter of ability; it's just a matter of time."

I noted to myself that Karen's "excuses"—as with most procrastinators—usually related to "not having enough time." I asked her, "When do you plan to get your degree?"

Again, Karen hesitated. "Well, I'd like to get it in two years," she said. "But I'd still rather accept an 'incomplete' and put up with the delay than settle for anything less than the best possible grade. Of course, the way I'm going now, I can see that it might take me another ten years!"

Ironically, when Karen does get an "A," it doesn't bolster her self-confidence or alleviate her tendency to "overdo" her schoolwork. "I always worry about failing the next class," she confessed. "I'm a serious student, I've done well in almost everything I've studied, but I still don't feel convinced that, yes, I'm competent and, yes, I am going to do a good job. All I can think about is how much I don't know and how many ways I might fail."

Procrastinating at Home

The methods Karen used to procrastinate at work and at school carried over into her home life as well. This was especially apparent in her housekeeping. "I admit I have high standards," she sighed. "It's a burden I wouldn't wish on my worst enemy. I think I have to do everything better than anyone else. My home is my showcase. I need to blow everyone away, show them how special I am."

Not being able to relax if there were dirty dishes in the sink or dust on the coffee table, Karen was forever busy doing small chores. And when there was a task that seemed intolerably difficult, given her perfectionist standards—such as organizing all the clutter in the attic, or planting a vegetable garden—she would avoid doing it, even though she couldn't avoid thinking about it. She might work a little bit on that task from time to time—moving a few boxes around in the attic or reading some more information about gardening—but she'd put off actually seeing the task through to completion, feeling overwhelmed that she couldn't do a "perfect" job.

Meanwhile, Karen's perfectionism was wreaking havoc in her relationship with her husband, Scott. She repeatedly fought with him over his messiness and his unwillingness (as she saw it) to do work that measured up to her high standards. She interpreted his perpetually casual ways of doing things to mean that he must not care about her, reasoning that if he *did* care about her, he would want to do what she wanted and therefore would change his ways.

Scott, in turn, accused Karen of being a "neat freak" and resorted to doing even less around the house than he otherwise might have done, so that it wouldn't appear as if he were co-operating with her maddening time- and energy-wasting habits. By the time she came to me for therapy, not only was she having more trouble than ever keeping up with housework, but her marriage was at an unprecedented breaking point.

When I asked Karen to talk about the first time she met Scott, she told me that she had liked him right away—partly because he was so easygoing. "He was cute, and funny, and I enjoyed the way he didn't take things so seriously—at least, not as seriously as I did. I also enjoyed the fact that all my girlfriends liked him. It made me feel secure."

Soon, however, Karen began to develop objections toward Scott—something that perfectionists are driven to do regarding anyone, or anything, they care about. "When Scott and I were alone during those first few months," she told me, "he would sometimes get quiet and withdrawn and do things I couldn't stand, like not shave, or eat food from cans with his fingers. That's when I began to waver about whether or not we should stay together and, later, whether or not we should marry."

Karen, in her own words, "drove Scott nuts" by putting off their engagement for months and then postponing their marriage date several times. Refusing to commit in relationships is typical of perfectionists: It's a form of procrastination that serves as a roadblock to real intimacy. When the perfectionist refuses either to accept or to reject the other person, the net effect is one of withholding. "I love you," the perfectionist is saying *"BUT. . . "* and the objections follow. Karen did finally take Scott as her husband, but she was continuing to delay actually accepting him as a separate person. Her unrealistically high standards were now applied not just to herself but to her husband as well.

Procrastinating over Self-Fulfillment

Karen admitted to me that the older she got, the more she realized that procrastination was costing her a long-cherished dream—to write a novel. When she was in her mid-twenties, she wrote a first draft of a story about two young lovers traveling through Europe, but she never had the courage to show it to anyone.

During the time that Karen was in therapy with me, she told a friend about the novel. But when her friend expressed a keen interest in reading it, Karen proceeded to tear apart the plot *and* her writing style in an effort to convince her friend that the manuscript was "not good enough for anyone to see." In making this kind of statement, perfectionists reveal their internal conflict between wanting approval and fearing it. Yes, Karen would have liked her friend to read the story and enjoy it (or Karen wouldn't have mentioned it at all); but she was also afraid that her friend's response would be negative. Thus, she isolated herself from getting someone else's viewpoint.

Closely associated with Karen's secret ambition to become a successful novelist was her not-so-secret desire to switch career fields from public relations to mass-market publishing. She often spoke to me about this, and I inferred from some of her other remarks that she talked about it frequently with her husband and her close friends. But she put off *doing* much about it. She often tore "position available" ads from the backs of literary magazines, but she seldom followed up on them. Once, she told me

about an employment opportunity at a local publishing house
that she wished she'd taken. When I asked her if she'd actually
pursued this opportunity, she replied, "Yes, but I kept putting
off calling, and when I finally did, the job had been filled. Just
my luck."

Sadly, Karen's "luck" was not to blame for her losing this
opportunity. Rather, it was her procrastination, fueled by her fear
that either the job wouldn't be perfect, or she wouldn't be perfect
in the job, or both.

How the Pattern Started

Very early in life, Karen began developing perfectionist habits
in response to her parents' and teachers' training. They always
impressed upon her the importance of "doing her best," and
longing to earn their approval, she eagerly complied. She wanted
to be "the perfect kid." Yet without realizing it, she was turning
herself into a precocious, obsessive little adult.

At home, she found it very difficult to get the kind of un-
qualified praise she craved. She recounted to me a time in third
grade when she got a 95 on her spelling test—the highest score
in her class. Her mother's first words when Karen showed her
the score were "What happened to those other five points?"
Karen was crushed. The following week, she brought home a
spelling test with a perfect 100 score, and her mother's reaction
was "Now, *that* is the kind of grade you should be getting all
the time!"

No doubt Karen's mother meant to inspire her. But instead
she only made it harder for Karen to celebrate her achievements
or to make realistic, commonsense judgments about how much
time and energy to put into what she did. Wanting to make sure
there were *no* grounds for disappointment, Karen always felt
obliged to do as much as possible.

At school, Karen's perfectionism was reinforced in a different, almost opposite way. She was so excessively praised for her high grades that she was led to believe that average grades were awful—as bad as outright failure. By the time she entered the sixth grade, she was an overly serious, nervous, and inefficient student. She didn't think of learning as fun or as something to nurture her development. She considered it to be a mission that reflected her worth.

To relieve the pressure involved in performing tasks at home and at school, Karen found herself procrastinating more and more often. Although she worked well beyond any reasonable point of conclusion on many of her projects, on others, especially ones that made her particularly anxious, she avoided doing anything until she absolutely had to do it. Secretly, she hoped that if she waited long enough, these tasks would disappear. When they didn't, she either stayed up very late, worked all weekend, or moaned and groaned until someone helped her out or took her off the hook.

An example of the latter scenario was Karen's experience with piano lessons at age twelve. When her parents first proposed the lessons, she was delighted; but her anticipation quickly turned to frustration when she couldn't get her fingers to move as skillfully over the keys as she wanted. Practicing a piece of music, she'd become enraged every time she hit a wrong note. After months of tears and tantrums, her parents stopped the lessons. In one respect, Karen was relieved: She no longer felt constrained to be a perfect pianist. But in another, more profound respect, she was upset with herself for having failed to master a difficult skill. As a result, she promised herself that henceforward she would stick to what she was sure she could do well.

Karen kept her resolution for a while, but in high school, it became impossible to sustain. The courses she was required to take were far more various and demanding than her previous school subjects had been; also, the criteria for earning a high grade were far more complex. Term papers and essay questions presented the stiffest challenges to her perfectionism. Unlike tests with clear "right" answers, each term paper or essay question was judged by a teacher according to subjective criteria. In effect, there was no predefined "perfect" answer.

Karen couldn't get comfortable with this kind of ambiguity. Time after time, she tortured herself trying to be sure she responded in exactly the way the teacher might want, and she never knew when enough was enough. Although she started many of her assignments right after they were given and kept working on them steadily, she didn't finish them until the early hours of the morning on the day they were due. She was forever trying to improve what she'd already done well.

Karen's teachers couldn't help but notice her grade-related anxiety. They told her that she was a good student, that she didn't need to worry so much, and that she really must relax more. Unfortunately, she had no idea how to follow their well-meaning advice.

Karen's parents took a different tack. "As I got older," she informed me, "my mother and father got more and more demanding. They kept telling me, 'Never settle for mediocrity. Whatever you do, put all you have behind it.' They would hold up famous people as models, saying, 'Look at the greats, the best of the best—the Einsteins, the Lincolns, the Mozarts of the world.' Even today, I still picture one of these greats looking at my work and ridiculing it: 'You think *this* is good? Is *this* really the best you can do?' "

Although Karen's parents were well-intentioned, they didn't appreciate the harm that resulted from their telling Karen to do her best *all the time*. They were offering their nervous, sensitive daughter only a trite generalization, with no specific strategies for accomplishing things effectively and efficiently in the real world and in real time. Their advice was similar to the advice financial experts often give for succeeding in the stock market: "Buy low; sell high." It's just too simplistic. It tells people *what* to do without telling them anything about *how* to do it. As far as Karen was concerned in her struggle with perfectionism and procrastination, she was getting well-meaning but uselessly vague counsel from *both* her teacher *and* her parents.

When I asked Karen how her parents dealt with failure, she lowered her head and was silent for a moment. Then, in a shaky voice, she murmured: "This is hard for me to talk about. You see, I was trained *not* to talk about it. When I was fourteen and first getting interested in boys, my sister, Marie, who was seventeen, got pregnant. Her high school boyfriend was the father. My parents were absolutely horrified! My father was cruel—he kept calling her 'stupid' and demanding that she get married. Her boyfriend was definitely not going to marry her, but my father wouldn't accept that, and my mother backed him up one hundred percent. Neither one of them tried to help her cope with her feelings or think through her options. To them, that would have meant condoning what she'd done. In the end, they just sent her away to have her baby and give it up for adoption. It became the family's shameful secret."

Karen was devastated; her need to be perfect intensified. She was now the only daughter who was expected to excel in college, to marry well, to shine at work, to do anything and everything to make up for the shame her sister had brought upon the family. It was a heavy weight for Karen to carry, one that she didn't know how to free herself of.

Changing the Pattern

Lifestyle changes, difficult for anyone to make, are particularly troublesome for perfectionists, who dread changing from a way of life that's very familiar to an untried way that might involve awkwardness, incompetence, or failure. Yet Karen realized that her procrastination problems would never be solved until she "unlearned" some of the burdensome perfectionism that lay behind those problems. Slowly and surely, we worked together toward changing some of the self-destructive ways she thought, spoke, and acted.

Before coming to me, Karen—in a typically perfectionist fashion—had assumed that therapeutic lifestyle changes needed to be extreme in nature and all-encompassing in scope in order to be effective. To her great surprise and relief, many of the techniques I recommended involved gradually adopting simple, almost mechanical changes in her day-to-day life.

For example, I'd noticed that Karen tended to use the word "should" a lot, as in "I should work on my report tonight," or "I know what I should have done." "Should" implies an ideal standard and an obligation to meet that standard—connotations that automatically reinforce a perfectionist point of view. As a means of shifting her speaking vocabulary away from language with the needlessly burdensome overtones and toward language connoting realism and choice, I suggested that she replace "should" in her conversations with "could." Thus, instead of (or immediately after) saying, for instance, "I *should* work on my report tonight," she was to say, "I *could* work on my report tonight." Virtually from the moment she started making this simple word substitution, she began talking in terms of choice ("I could do it this way, or that way") rather than excuses ("I should do it this way, *BUT* . . .").

Other strategies that I thought might benefit Karen—and that did, in fact, work very well—required more effort on her part. Nevertheless, they still involved specific, easy-to-do activities that she could engage in repeatedly over time. Thus, she could easily envision, control, measure, and enjoy her rate of change.

For example, I advised her to practice deliberately making a small "mistake" in the way she did a certain task, so that she could notice how it felt and what—if anything—happened as a consequence. The first "deliberate mistake" she tried, on her own initiative, was to make her bed with the spread wrong side up. She told me that the bedspread looked weird to her in its "wrong" position and that each time she looked at it, she felt a tremendous urge to "fix" it. Yet she let it remain and grew more and more aware as the day went on that it just didn't matter. Her husband never even noticed it! The next day, when she turned it over, she no longer attached quite so much importance to the need to do it "just right." Thus, she'd knocked one more time- and energy-consuming chip off her perfectionism.

Karen's next "deliberate mistake" was a bigger risk for her, because I suggested that she make it at work. What mistake could she dare to make deliberately in an environment that she, as a perfectionist, considered to be so important? Together, we devised a plan.

In Karen's department, the staff was supposed to sign in when they arrived and sign out when they left for the day. Karen decided that her deliberate mistake at work would be to neglect to sign in. This type of mistake was so out of character for her that she was literally sweating with anxiety when she arrived at the office building; but she defiantly walked right past the sign-in sheet without even looking at it. She could feel her heart pounding as she sat down at her desk—it was as if she had just shoplifted something. After a few moments, though, she got down to business as usual. It wasn't until just before lunch that the departmental receptionist came into Karen's office with the sign-in sheet and said, "Karen, it looks like you forgot to sign in this morning." Karen feigned surprise, signed the sheet, and that was that. Recounting the incident to me, Karen exclaimed, "You know what really shocked me? After a short time, I'd forgotten all about not signing in, until the receptionist showed up in my office!"

HOW TO STOP BEING
A PERFECTIONIST PROCRASTINATOR

I chose to discuss Karen's story at length because the first, vitally important step any perfectionist procrastinator can take toward overcoming his or her problems is to identify them. If you scored high on perfectionism in the Chapter 1 quiz, you no doubt recognized some of your own self-defeating patterns in Karen's story. Now you need to think about your own present and past experiences more specifically and identify the different ways in which your perfectionism has caused you to procrastinate. As a beginning, try this self-assessment exercise:

1. Recall at least two different occasions when you *spent an excessive amount of time and energy doing something* in an effort to get it done perfectly. (If you can, try to identify at least one time when you did not, in fact, get the task done despite your excessive effort.) Then, for each incident, ask yourself these questions:
   • Why, specifically, did I want to do a perfect job?
   • Aside from satisfying the need I felt to do a perfect job, was it actually necessary to spend so much time and energy? If so, why? If not, why not?
   • Aside from anticipating the possibility of doing a perfect job, did I actually enjoy spending so much time and energy? If so, why? If not, why not?

2. Recall at least two times when you *avoided doing something altogether—or until the last minute*—because you were afraid you wouldn't do a perfect job. For each incident, ask yourself these questions:

- Why, specifically, was I so afraid of not doing well?
- How, specifically, did I go about avoiding this task?
- What feelings did I have while I was avoiding this task?
- What happened as a result of my avoidance?

As you go on to examine more closely the specific problems you've had as a perfectionist procrastinator, you'll gain more and more understanding of how those problems have interfered with your happiness and productivity. Further, you'll become increasingly motivated to do something about them.

Offered on the following pages are effective strategies for overcoming your perfectionist procrastination in the three major ways that you express it: thinking, speaking, and acting. Try all the guidelines over a period of at least six weeks, but remember not to be too compulsive (a perfectionist tendency). Change happens slowly and gradually. Be patient and dedicated in your efforts to apply the guidelines, and you will soon notice many positive differences in your life.

CHANGING HOW YOU THINK

1. *Practice creative visualization.*

Creative visualization involves first relaxing your body and your mind, and then deliberately "seeing" with your mind's eye images that are refreshing, positive, and constructive. These mental images can serve to counteract the negative ones that get involuntarily triggered by your "single-minded" tendency toward perfectionism and procrastination. Creative visualization can be especially helpful for you at times when you feel tense as a result of your perfectionism and/or procrastination.

On the next page is a creative-visualization exercise that

I developed specifically for my clients who are perfectionist procrastinators. Before trying it out, read it all the way through several times, until you feel you know it pretty well. Remember, you don't have to do it perfectly! As long as you get the gist of it, you'll do fine.

When you're ready to do the visualization, assume a comfortable position somewhere that's quiet, dimly lit, and free from distractions or interruptions. Some people like to lie down on the floor with their legs straight and slightly apart, and their arms extended loosely at an angle from their sides. Others would rather relax in a comfortable chair or couch.

Then, after you've settled into your position, silently repeat each guideline to yourself as you remember it. Go all the way through the visualization scenario at a slow, relaxed pace. Make sure to allow at least a minute of quiet visualization time between instructions. The entire exercise is designed to take approximately fifteen to twenty minutes.

You can also record the guidelines on an audiotape, so that you can play the tape back whenever you want to repeat the imagery. While recording, speak in a slow, soothing voice, allowing approximately a minute of silence between instructions.

An alternative method is to have someone read the guidelines to you in the same relaxing manner. Choose someone with whom you feel comfortable, and let this person practice reading the guidelines once all the way through before you begin.

Visualization for the Perfectionist Procrastinator

(1) Close your eyes and take a few deep breaths to relax your body—inhaling slowly through your nose, then exhaling slowly through your mouth. Let go of any tension or tight-

ness you are experiencing in your body. Allow the thoughts and cares of the day to drift away, leaving your body feeling light, your mind feeling empty.

(2) In this relaxed mode, picture the one main problem that is worrying you: the task or activity that you keep working on too much, or that you keep putting off. See a definite image in your mind that represents this problem.

(3) Keeping this image in your mind, let yourself feel all the troublesome emotions that are associated with this problem. Be aware of how many different ways this problem frustrates you. Notice how your body responds. Slowly increase the muscular tension in your arms and legs as you let your anxiety level rise.

(4) Now picture this image—the one that represents your problem—slowly shrinking. And as it shrinks, imagine the anxieties and the troublesome emotions in your mind and your body gradually lessen. See the image getting smaller and smaller, until it's nothing more than a tiny black ball.

(5) Notice that you are now holding this small black ball in the palm of your hand. All of the harmful emotions are no longer in your body or your mind. They are all contained inside this ball, which you are holding firmly in your grasp.

(6) Picture yourself still holding this ball in your hand, but now you are sitting comfortably under a tree in a beautiful meadow on a warm spring day. You can feel the soft grass beneath your body. You can feel the warmth of the sun and see soft white clouds floating across the sky.

(7) Still sitting under this tree, imagine the small black ball in your hand turning into a helium balloon. You open

your hand and release the balloon, watching it rise up, up, up into the sky and disappear from view. All you see is the blue sky and the white clouds going by.

(8) Now you look back at your hand, and there's a small pink heart lying there. You press this heart to your chest and feel it pass into your body easily and magically. Imagine the heart inside you, slowly and comfortably expanding and filling you with a sense of peace and well-being.

(9) Now hear the nurturing voice of the heart telling you, "You're just fine. I accept you—exactly the way you are. If you take things easy, you will get things done. You will find a way. It doesn't have to be perfect. You don't have to be perfect." As you take in the warmth and acceptance of your heart, feel your body relaxing, your mind feeling peaceful and serene.

(10) Continue to relax, enjoying the way you feel. Notice how calm you are when you feel okay about yourself and about the things you do. Take as much time as you need, and whenever you are ready, slowly open your eyes. With your eyes open, say something nurturing to yourself, and believe it with all your heart.

2. *Acknowledge that perfectionism is* your *problem.*

Most perfectionists interpret their problems as being "out there." They tell themselves, "Why should I lower *my* standards? If the world worked the way it should, there wouldn't be so much trouble." The truth is that perfectionists themselves don't work the way they think they should. Their tendency to procrastinate is only one way in which they fall short of the perfection they claim. But even more to the point, the world is definitely not going to change to suit the perfectionist.

You have very limited control—if any—over how others live their lives. Thus, if you are highly frustrated by things like your spouse's sloppiness, your friend's lateness, or the traffic jam created by all the other drivers, don't waste a lot of energy expecting them to change. Recognize that *your* perfectionism is a big part of the problem; and if you want a happier, more productive life, it's up to *you* to change.

3. *Strive for excellence rather than perfection.*

Perfection—defined as "the absolute," "the condition of being flawless," "the most desirable state that can be imagined"—is a highly elusive, if not impossible, standard to envision, much less achieve. And most likely, no two people will agree on what constitutes "perfection" in a given situation. What does a "perfect" woman's body look like? How does the "perfect" father behave? What's the "perfect" job for a person with your talents and lifestyle?

Compared to perfection, *excellence*—defined as "very good of its kind" or "high-quality performance"—is a much clearer, more practical target to aim for and to achieve. You can be an excellent student without having to achieve a perfect 100—or even an "A"—on every assignment, and you can be an excellent batter with a .375 batting average, which is very far from a perfect 1.0!

4. *Focus on what's realistic rather than what's ideal.*

When you think about performing a certain task, resist the immediate impulse to think of the *best possible way* that the task could be performed. Instead, think of *several possible ways* it could be done, and then choose the one that's the most realistic, given the time and resources available and your own past experience.

Similarly, when you think about the various things you

could do over a given period of time (an afternoon, a week-end, a month, whatever), avoid imagining *all the things you could possibly do* in that time, assuming everything goes the way you want it to go. Instead, ask yourself *what's realistic for you to expect to do,* given your own past experience and the fact that some aspects of what you're considering will be out of your control.

Keep in mind that some things may not have to be done especially well—they may simply have to be done. Try to identify those routine household or clerical tasks that you can perform in a "less than excellent" manner without causing any real problems. Your goal for these tasks can be just to get them out of the way, rather than to do them well. If you continue to think that you have to do *everything* well, then *everything* becomes a burden.

5. Practice self-acceptance rather than self-condemnation.

Make a conscious effort to be kinder toward yourself. Too much self-criticism can be paralyzing. If you're worried about doing something that you're not good at, or if a proj-ect isn't going well for you, don't make matters worse by berating yourself. Instead, try to be positive and self-motivating, saying to yourself things like, "You can do it," or "Keep going forward—things will get better."

If you're not satisfied with something you did, or if you experience a setback, don't beat yourself up. Remember that trying and failing to achieve a goal is part of testing one's limits—and, ultimately, expanding them. Whenever you have what you perceive to be a failure, say to yourself, "This type of thing happens to everyone from time to time, and it's a chance to learn something. It doesn't mean I'm a failure as a person—it means I'm on my way to being a success. I just need to keep moving forward."

6. *Avoid "all or nothing" thinking.*

Perfectionist procrastinators are inclined to think in terms of extremes. For example, they'll say to themselves, "If I don't do a perfect job, I've failed"—which implies the extremes "perfection" and "failure"—instead of, "It's not important that this job be done perfectly, just that it be done well, and there are a number of ways to do that."

Try working consciously to avoid or correct this type of extremism in *any* thoughts you may have. For example, don't be quick to judge a new person you meet as either "wonderful" or "awful." Instead, be more descriptive rather than evaluative—"I enjoyed/didn't enjoy being with that person because . . . " Don't limit your options about how to tackle tasks by thinking, "The only way I can do it is . . ." Instead, prod yourself to be more open and flexible, by thinking: "Let's see, what are my options? One way I could do it is . . . Or I could . . . Or I could . . ."

CHANGING HOW YOU SPEAK

1. *Change your "should"s to "could"s.*

When applied to yourself, the word "should" indicates a command that originates from outside yourself. It suggests that you bear some sort of responsibility you're reluctant to fulfill, as in "I should take care of that right away," or "I should change the last part of my speech so it's even better." In effect, the statement says, "I feel somehow obligated to do this, but I'm not quite ready to declare that I *will* do this."

To avoid imposing unnecessary pressure on yourself, strike the word "should" from your vocabulary and substitute "could," as in "I *could* take care of that right away," or "I *could* change the last part of my speech so it's even better." The word "could" reminds you that you *always* have the power to choose. Then, when you've made your choice, say a good, firm, motivational "I *will*."

2. *Change your "have to"s to "want to"s.*

How often have you heard yourself saying something like, "I have to be home by 6 P.M.," or "I have to do this project well so I can start earning some more money"? Whenever you use the phrase "have to," which implies coercion, you are making your assignment all the more onerous to fulfill. You are declaring out loud that you are undertaking this action only because someone or something is making you do so. In fact, it's usually only *you* that's applying the pressure on yourself. Instead of saying "have to," say "want to." Give yourself an incentive to act, rather than a lash of the whip!

3. *Change your "must"s to "choose to"s.*

The word "must" is another form of coercion—only it's one degree more forceful and more burdensome, especially when spoken aloud. "I must do this project before noon" is even more likely to provoke resentment and resistance than "I should/have to do this project before noon." Replacing "must" with "choose to" (as in "I choose to do this project before noon") will help you recognize that you do have a choice in the matter. As you change your speech patterns, you will realize that not everything "must" be done the way you initially think it "must" be done. Paradoxically, as you let go of some of your self-imposed demands, you may find yourself working much more effectively and efficiently.

4. *Avoid using extreme words in your conversation.*

As a perfectionist, you set extreme standards; and as a procrastinator, you tend to work too much or too little. To temper your overall tendency toward extremism, try to avoid using superlatives in your conversations. For example, instead of using the adjective "perfect" to describe something, substitute the adjective "interesting," "informative," or "valuable." Instead of claiming something was "the worst thing I could have done," describe it as "a simple mistake."

CHANGING HOW YOU ACT

1. *Give yourself a time limit for completing a task.*

Time is finite. We each have twenty-four hours in a day to get things done, and a hefty number of those hours need to be spent sleeping and eating. Take out some more time for dealing with the unexpected, and there's only a very limited amount left for other activities. As a perfectionist procrastinator, you need to make a special effort to remind yourself of this fact: If you spend too much time on one project in an effort to do a perfect job, it is certain to have a negative effect on other tasks you want to accomplish.

To make sure that you devote an appropriate amount of time to each task, you need to develop a "time budget," with deadlines and milestones for each task. Don't get caught thinking or saying something like, "I'll do this repair *as soon as possible*," or I'll have this project finished *sometime* next week." Instead, review your overall schedule and assign a specific time frame to each task. In determining these time frames, consider past experiences with similar tasks, then give yourself just ten percent extra "slack" time to allow for unexpected delays or interruptions.

2. *If you're not able to set time limits for yourself, ask others to help you set them.*

As a perfectionist and a procrastinator, you may not always be the best judge of how to spend your time. If you're confused, get some help from someone who may be more qualified—or at least more objective.

This strategy works well even for small things, like getting dressed for a party. If you can't seem to pull yourself away from the mirror at home because you're ambivalent about what you see, and if there's someone else in the house whose opinion you respect, don't hesitate to ask this person, "How do I look?" If this person says, "Just fine!" accept that answer, and get moving!

3. *Make a daily "to do" list that's short and practical.*

As a perfectionist procrastinator, you need to guard against either trying to do everything at once or concentrating all your attention on only one thing, to the exclusion of everything else you need—or want—to do. In other words, you should get your priorities in order.

Make a short, practical "to do" list for each day—either the night before or first thing in the morning. Don't try to write everything on it that you'd ideally like to do, or you'll be putting too much pressure on yourself. Instead, just write the things that are most important for you to do—your top priorities. And don't write too many top priorities. Each and every day, you need to allow yourself some "down" time to relax and enjoy life!

4. *Get others involved, letting them do things their way.*

Perfectionist procrastinators often wind up taking on too many chores and obligations in the first place, certain that they can handle them better than others can. Then, as they start handling those chores and obligations, they invest more time in some of them than is necessary and avoid working on others until the last minute, when they're forced to make a superhuman effort.

As a perfectionist procrastinator, you need to overcome the fantasy that you can—and should—do everything all by yourself. Instead, you need to learn to seek help before you're feeling pressured by too much work. Periodically, look over all the things that you feel you need to do at home, at work, and elsewhere, and identify individual tasks (or parts of tasks) that could be done by other people. Then start delegating some of your workload to the appropriate people.

Just be sure when you turn over *responsibility* for a task to another person that you also give that person *authority* over the task. As a perfectionist, you may hate to give up any of your control, thinking, "If I want the job done right, I have to do it myself." However, if you delegate a job to someone else, it's unfair to expect that person to do it exactly your way. It's best to give people an appropriate amount of freedom to do it according to their own best judgment.

5. *Make one deliberate mistake every day.*

There's no better way to change your perfectionist habits than to practice being imperfect, so that you deliberately accept the experience and thereby discover what it can teach you. Linger five minutes longer at home to make yourself late for an appointment. Leave your desk half messy for a whole week. Let a grammatical error in an office memo go uncorrected. Contrary to what you may believe in your heart of hearts, you'll find that making mistakes need not mean the end of the world. Every now and then, a mistake—and a sense of a humor about it—might even make your world a more comfortable, relaxing place to inhabit!

7. *Reward yourself for your achievements.*

Many perfectionists can't enjoy themselves even when they've accomplished what they set out to do. They won't let themselves celebrate: There's always something else waiting to be done, and they feel they should get started on it as soon as they can.

To make sure that you do take pleasure in your successes, commit yourself to a reward system. It doesn't matter whether the reward you give yourself for a specific accomplishment is big (for example, a vacation), medium (a new piece of clothing), or small (an ice-cream sundae), as long as you give yourself something!

8. *Learn the value of simply "being" instead of "doing."*

Many perfectionists think of life strictly in terms of what they have or haven't done. They don't give sufficient consideration—and therefore time—to the quality of their day-to-day existence, to the satisfaction they can derive from simply being, without having to do anything.

As much as you can, allow yourself time off to relax and to savor the world around you. Sit back, or take a walk, and do nothing at all but enjoy your own aliveness.

Chapter 3

The Dreamer Procrastinator

". . . <u>But</u> I hate dealing with all those bothersome details!"

The capacity to dream—to develop idealistic hopes, schemes, and scenarios as we go about our day-to-day lives—is one of our greatest assets. In our dreams, anything can happen. And only by returning to our dreams again and again can we come to appreciate the wide range of things that are possible, so that we can inspire ourselves to reach even higher than our logical mind contemplates.

The trick is in not forgetting the *reaching* part. Eleanor Roosevelt spoke wisely when she said, "The future belongs to those who believe in the beauty of their dreams." Some people, however, have trouble progressing beyond simply *dreaming*. For them, the future can be very slow in arriving, if it arrives at all, and their capacity to dream can turn into a liability instead of a gift.

These people I call "dreamer procrastinators." They have an especially strong desire to linger in the imaginary land of promising ideas as long as they can, and an equally strong aversion to applying themselves to real-world demands. They're full of excuses to buy more dream time, the most common one being "I know what I want to do, *BUT* I hate dealing with all those bothersome details!"

At one end of the dreamer-procrastinator spectrum is Tabitha, who fits the popular conception of a dreamer. In her late twen-

ties, she leads a free-spirited lifestyle that includes some painting, occasional modeling, frequent consultations with psychics,
weekly lottery tickets, and lots of "hanging out." Over the past
ten years, she's had countless short, unchallenging work assignments and several long, aimless periods of unemployment. Pub-
licly, she claims that she doesn't want to "sell out" by getting a
steady job or pursuing a career. Privately, she feels it would
involve far too much hard work.

Tabitha's conversation revolves around speculative matters
more than actual occurrences and spins swiftly from subject to
subject. Sometimes it's very entertaining, even fascinating to her
listeners; other times, she appears scatterbrained or phony. She
also lacks focus in the way she manages her time and energy.
When close friends gently pressure her to be more realistic about
deadlines, commitments, or responsibilities, she laughs them off.
Indeed, she seems perpetually adrift.

At the other end of the dreamer-procrastinator spectrum is
Margie, a sensitive, caring social-services supervisor who is in
her mid-forties. Superficially, she appears to be a heroic-scale
"doer," on a mission to save the world. Time after time, she
rescues clients from near disaster; and she's constantly decrying
the injustices of life to her husband, Gene, or anyone else who
will listen.

A closer examination shows that Margie is in fact a dreamer
procrastinator. Although she may throw herself into the big rescue projects at work, she finds it hard to attend to the simpler,
day-by-day tasks that represent the bulk of her job. Occasionally,
without realizing it, her lack of attention to routine matters actually creates the crisis that requires the rescue and appeals to
her sense of drama.

At home, Margie counts upon Gene to take care of the practical side of their life together, just as she counts upon staff
members to handle the "boring" office details. Unfortunately, her

reliance upon Gene extends to many personal needs, with which she remains dreamily out of touch. She doesn't interpret this type of dependency as unfair: Why shouldn't other people help her out, since she does "everything" for others? Sometimes she resents the success and happiness of people who seem selfish compared to her. Why, she wonders, is she, the good one, so often unappreciated, unrewarded, and unsatisfied?

Like Tabitha, Margie suffers a great deal of frustration and self-doubt because of the gap between her fantasies and her real life. Despite their apparent differences, both women are dreamer procrastinators, exhibiting all four of the basic characteristics of that style:

1. *Dreamer procrastinators desperately want life to be easy and pleasant, so they automatically recoil from anything that might be difficult or distressing.*

   Dreamers try as much as they can to coast through the stresses and strains of day-to-day life in a dreamy state of disengagement. Imagining the ideal life to be one that is comfortable and non-threatening, they continually strive to "feel good." In the process, they lose sight of who they *really* are and therefore how they *really* feel. No wonder any deep, enduring satisfaction eludes them!

   We see this trait most obviously in the way Tabitha lives. She resists the everyday world, preferring an alternative world that is somehow better, freer, less problematic. She's avoided reality for so long that she's lost her sense of perspective—exaggerating the difficulty and pain of doing things that "ordinary" people do all the time, such as holding down a steady job or building a meaningful career.

   This comfort orientation manifests itself more subtly in the way Margie functions. Although a non-dreamer might be intimidated by having to play the role of "grand res-

cuer," Margie, the dreamer, finds it pleasurable to act out
—at least, every now and then. What troubles her is
focusing on "the daily grind." In her thoughts about her
own life as well as her clients' lives, she is committed to
the notion that *everything* should be easy and pleasant, and
anything that threatens that state is bad. She resists accepting the fact that a real, substantial life brings with it a
certain number of non-dream-like chores, problems, hard-
ships, and responsibilities that are necessary—and even
worthwhile—to address.

2. *Because dreamer procrastinators live so much in their fantasies, they tend to be passive rather than active.*

Dreamer procrastinators often weave grandiose fantasies
about themselves to compensate for their lack of solid
achievement in real life. In this they resemble Walter Mitty,
of humorist James Thurber's well-known story "The Secret
Life of Walter Mitty."

Longing to exchange his wishy-washy, "bungler" identity
as a husband and city dweller for some grander role in life,
Mitty spends all his mental energy translating small daily
events into self-ennobling fantasies. Revving his car en-
gine, he daydreams of being a heroic war pilot. The sight
of a hospital building triggers a vision of himself as a bril-
liant surgeon. When he hears a news vendor shout a head-
line about a trial, he imagines he is a celebrated trial
lawyer. Repeatedly out of touch with what's happening
around him, he remains a wishy-washy bungler.

In her job as a social-services supervisor, Margie occasionally functions as a grand rescuer, but her existence as
a whole feels dormant, lifeless, unfulfilling, as if she were
continually waiting for something to wake her up. Tabitha
conceives of herself as a uniquely gifted "child of the cos-

mos" but—understandably—can't find a way to translate that vague conception into action. Thus, she either seeks more material for her fantasies (another spiritual pathway, a new prophecy from a psychic) or sinks into the purer form of mental procrastination known technically as omphaloskepsis—"the contemplation of one's navel."

3. *Because dreamer procrastinators tend to be vague, paying little attention to facts and details, it's difficult for them to focus on—or perform—specific tasks.*

   Dreamer procrastinators instinctively prefer thinking (or the kind of talking that's "thinking out loud") to doing. The former allows for much more imaginative freedom and imprecision than the latter. Over time, they can start to confuse the two, believing they've accomplished something just because they've thought or talked a lot about it.

   This confusion characterizes much of their relationship to the outside world. Instead of seeing *specific* tasks to be fulfilled, they see *general* things to think and fantasize about. Instead of getting around to performing tasks, they spend their time spinning out their task-avoiding thoughts and fantasies. Thus Tabitha loses focus on the real-world dimension of her life, and thus Margie finds it difficult to manage her day-to-day life more effectively.

4. *Dreamer procrastinators think of themselves as special people for whom fate will intervene, making hard work and efficiency unnecessary.*

   Living such a large portion of their lives inside their own heads, dreamer procrastinators tend to become narcissistic. In many cases, this narcissism is fed by outsiders, who can be especially attracted to a dreamer's creativity and charm. Such a dreamer procrastinator is led to feel that he or she is uniquely fated to succeed and doesn't need to be as concerned with practical activities as other people are.

Both Tabitha and Margie exhibit this characteristic of *waiting* for their dreams to come true, instead of acting on their own behalf to make them come true. There is something childlike about their separation from real life, with the distinction that children are *naturally* immature, while they are *willfully* immature.

The writer Wendy Wasserstein refers to this latter state of being as "Peter Pannery," the refusal to lead an adult life. In a recent article, she courageously admitted her own tendency toward Peter Pannery, despite being in her "fourth decade": "I've been waiting till I grow up to officially commit to a grown-up apartment. . . .Even though I've lived in a glamorous, four-room, park-view apartment for a year and a half, I'm only subletting a grown-up life. . . ." ("Getting a Real Grown-Up Life Can Wait," *The New York Times*, February 9, 1995.)

In all four of the ways described above, Tabitha and Margie seem to be subletting their lives instead of owning them. Let's probe more deeply into this kind of half-life by considering the history of a former client of mine whom I'll call Jeff.

JEFF: THE DREAMER PROCRASTINATOR

At age thirty-three, Jeff already felt he'd made it to the top. He had a loving wife, an exciting new job as the "idea man" in a prestigious industrial design firm, and a mind that never seemed to stop working. His employers were enormously impressed with the projects he proposed. He was going to create a chair capable of giving each user a uniquely customized massage, a combination phone-wristwatch that would revolutionize the telecommunications industry, and a breakthrough technology for turning recycled glass and aluminum into kitchen countertops and bathroom vanities.

Then came the first significant deadline. The firm's partners gathered in the executive conference room to review the plans for the massage chair—a showcase product they wanted to unveil at a major trade fair a month later. But the chair prototype wasn't ready. In fact, their acclaimed "idea" man had advanced very little beyond the idea stage. He'd researched other types of massage chairs but had yet to analyze their specifications as closely as was necessary. He'd interviewed several potential dealers and users but had not gotten around to conducting the focus groups that the firm required. He hadn't even arrived at a final cost figure, offering only a ballpark estimate.

His boss watched in horror and disbelief as Jeff simply reiterated his initial concept to the firm's partners, as if he felt that recharging their interest in the project was sufficient for the moment. Afterward, the partners huddled and made two quick decisions: There would be no mention at the trade fair of any wondrous new massage chair, and their resident genius was fired.

This worst-ever setback in Jeff's life brought him to me for counseling. My first impression was positive: Here sat a charming, likable, upbeat man who appeared to be a go-getter temporarily down on his luck. But as he continued to talk, I began to wonder how realistic he was. His speech was full of hyperboles—all the things he intended to do were "big," "important," or "unprecedented." And yet his grandiose plans didn't seem supported or counterbalanced by any specific activities. What, exactly, did these many great ideas add up to? Was there any genuine substance behind the fabulous image?

The succeeding months in therapy uncovered a real self behind his facade that had repeatedly been confused, embarrassed, and defeated by discrepancies between his dreams and his true-life experiences. It turned out that Jeff had been fired from several jobs for the same reason that he'd been fired from the design firm—a failure to follow up words with deeds.

Each time this happened, Jeff would tell himself and others that he wasn't being fired, he was being "let go," and the problem wasn't him but the poor economy, or his boss's lack of understanding, or the impossibility of the task he was given. Deep inside, however, during his most honest moments of introspection, he knew that something must be wrong with the way he functioned. He simply didn't feel "real," which in turn made him feel ashamed. After examining his life patterns more closely during the course of our work together, he could finally define what had been troubling him: He was a dreamer procrastinator.

Procrastinating at Work

The sheer number of jobs Jeff had held in his relatively short life testified to his "dreamer" tendency to put off committing himself to a real, solid career. He enjoyed the "all-things-possible" aspect of new ventures but tired of these ventures quickly as they aged and demanded more and more practical implementation.

Each day at work, Jeff would drift from distraction to distraction. He even invited interruptions, like phone calls, drop-in visitors, or sudden errands, preferring the novelty of the unexpected break to the tedium of the ongoing task at hand. His friends and colleagues thought of him as a very conscientious, nurturing person because he repeatedly told them, "I'm always available if you need to talk or need a helping hand, no matter how busy I am." They didn't realize that his offers of help were actually pleas for distraction from his own work.

In general, Jeff's work energy tended to be scattered and undisciplined. On some level, he liked it that way and abhorred the notion of operating with more logic and consistency. If he had an unanticipated hour of "downtime" on his hands, he'd fritter it away looking at magazines or shuffling the papers on his desk, instead of using it to catch up on an overdue assignment. He'd telephone suppliers or clients only when he felt like it, even if it was the most unlikely time to reach them—like Friday at 4 P.M. If they weren't there, he'd often neglect to leave a message on their voice mail, which would ultimately waste even more time.

When it came to devising work strategies, Jeff would choose fun over efficiency every time. If he needed to plan a get-together with a group of colleagues to determine a marketing campaign, he'd arrange a three-hour lunch-plus-gabfest, instead of a two-hour meeting in the conference room. If he needed to refresh his understanding of a certain design style, he'd spend an entire afternoon watching entertaining but superficial videotapes rather than apply himself to an hour's intensive book study.

Thinking himself to be an exceptionally creative person (as well he might, so prodigious a dreamer was he), Jeff belittled many of his job-related tasks, considering them too simplistic or mundane for his "special" kind of attention. Thus, they never got done, or they got done poorly at the last minute. Other job-related tasks he would inflate out of all proportion, because of his tendency toward grandiose thinking.

For example, when Jeff was fresh out of college, he landed a good entry-level job as an assistant designer in an architectural firm, and one of his first assignments was to put together a directory of local organizations that in-house personnel could use. In his head, he quickly turned this relatively easy, short-term assignment into a gigantic project, with related national listings, supplementary reference features, and cross-indexed appendixes. It became such a large, complicated effort that he didn't get it down on paper in the time allotted, nor did he fault himself for not doing so. After the inevitable reprimand from his boss, he complained to a colleague, "How could they expect just one person to get all that work done in such a short time! They must have been dreaming!" They weren't, but he most assuredly was.

Several failed jobs later, Jeff decided to go into business for himself. His interior design showroom, at least, was a dream come true. People raved about it, and they were also enthusiastic about him, thanks to his charisma. "A born salesman," they called him. Maybe, but he was a lousy businessman.

Jeff always managed to hold on to a few prominent and well-paying customers—just enough to fuel his fantasy of being a "boy wonder" on the fast track—but he couldn't sustain the business. He just wasn't able to focus on the everyday facts and figures that were the crucial elements in keeping it alive: this nuts-and-bolts cost of maintaining his "dream" showroom, the month-to-month sales volume that he needed to generate in order to meet his expense deadlines, the line-by-line details of the contracts he signed.

Nor could Jeff stick to the truth when he communicated business information to his staff: It was always wrapped up in the fancy packaging of his wishful thinking and self-inflating delusions. Eventually, his secretary, at her own insistence, started accompanying him to meetings with clients, just so that she could be sure about what was agreed to and what was not. Despite initially liking him for his optimism and kindness, she and the entire staff grew to loathe his "What—me worry?" attitude. "If we lose the account," he would say in his typical "dare to dream" fashion whenever trouble brewed, "another account will come along to take its place." Finally, all the accounts stopped coming along, and he lost his business.

"It was a terrible time for small independents," Jeff told his subsequent employers at the industrial design firm. In his mind, the vague "it" took the blame for the failure, and his own specific identity became submerged in the abstract category "small independents."

Procrastinating in His Personal Life

At the time Jeff first came to see me, he felt he was failing in his personal as well as his professional life. Five months earlier, when he'd just landed his "big, important" job at the design firm, he'd spent more than $50,000 on an executive wardrobe and a luxury car. Unfortunately, he couldn't afford to do this, but he rarely let facts pin him down. In this case, he had to have the clothes and the car, among other expensive accoutrements, to provide tangible support for his private notion that he was a rising star.

Jeff went deeply into debt, extending his credit (and that of his wife, Lisa) to the breaking point. When the bills began pouring in, he didn't pay them. He put them in a drawer and out of his mind. As a dreamer procrastinator, he convinced himself that he didn't need to pay them right away, or to start saving money to pay them later; he could count on quick success in the future to bring him all the money he needed and more.

Beset by creditors, Lisa was forced to snoop through Jeff's papers to find out just how precarious their financial situation was. When she found out, she was filled with rage, not so much at her husband's spending all that money without telling her as at his being unwilling to take their increasing debt as a serious matter. Jeff agreed with her that he ought to be handling money matters in a more responsible manner, and he appeared sincerely contrite and remorseful, but that agreement and appearance did not translate into action for long. As Jeff let the money problems get out of hand once again, Lisa felt compelled against her will to take them over herself, and she strongly resented it.

A similar type of equivocation had kept them from starting a family. Lisa definitely wanted to have children, and Jeff said he did, even spinning humorous fantasies for Lisa about "little Jethro and Jethrine," but he kept putting the decision off. He told Lisa they could have kids "anytime," so why not wait just a while longer, until he was well established in his career?

Now, after four years of "a while longer" Lisa was thoroughly disillusioned. She had heard what she called his "Mr. Big" pitch countless times and couldn't bring herself to believe it anymore. She told this to Jeff in no uncertain terms, she thought, but Jeff kept on pitching it as if he hadn't heard her. Completely frustrated, she could only lash out at him. "I'm sick and tired of waiting!" she'd scream. "If you really do want children, let's start *now!*" "Have faith," he'd reply. "One day it *is* going to happen, I promise." He seemed incapable of realizing that "one day" is no specific day at all.

As for everyday household life, Jeff behaved much the way he did at work, only worse. His grandiose self-image gave him a heightened sense of entitlement, and so his prevailing attitude around the house was, "I work hard all day at the office. I should be able to come home and relax!" He was loving and good-natured toward Lisa, but he made it subtly known that performing routine chores or repairs was "beneath" his dignity. He'd put them off to watch a football game on TV or to practice his golf swing, saying that there would be plenty of time to do the "drudge" work, but that time didn't seem to come around very often.

Whenever Jeff took on—or was presented with—a more worthy household challenge, his dreaming mind would inflate it into such a monstrous superproject that he was almost certain never to get it started or, if he did, never to complete it. Once, he told Lisa that he would refinish an antique chest of drawers they were considering buying for their living room. In fact, his announcement of this intention was the final argument for their buying it, since its finish was almost worn off. After fussing around with the job for a while, purchasing brushes and looking at finishing samples, he decided that the whole living room would have to be repainted, and major pieces of living room furniture replaced, to do justice to the refinishing job. The ever-enlarging task soon became overwhelming, and so it was abandoned, the antique chest with its worn-off finish left to sit in the attic.

Jeff's dreamer-style optimism and good humor usually took these minor setbacks in stride, but they often irritated his wife and friends. One of his most annoying traits was his failure to anticipate contingencies. He would put off buying plane tickets for a vacation until the last minute, when he was compelled to pay premium fare. It didn't seem to bother him, but it rattled Lisa, who, after all, wound up being the bill-keeper. It also seemingly never occurred to Jeff that a family emergency might arise while he was away from home, that an appliance he was depending upon might not work, that people he needed to reach might not be readily available, or that he might be tired or sick on the upcoming "busy" weekend he was envisioning. This obliviousness left him with little scope and few resources to handle the unexpected, and it frequently left his wife and friends in the lurch.

Learning to Procrastinate as a Child and a Student

Jeff's parents played a key role—directly and indirectly—in his becoming a dreamer procrastinator. When he was fourteen, his father, a taxicab driver, was severely injured in a car accident, and afterward could work only sporadically. Jeff's mother took a job in a factory to help support the family. Finding it hard to deal with a reduced standard of living, his father constantly dreamed of someday taking his family to Florida for "a vacation of a lifetime"—a dream that Jeff took quite seriously—but was disappointed each time the family couldn't afford to go.

As Jeff grew older, he spent a lot of time daydreaming about the better life he was going to make for his family once he struck it rich. He envisioned the nice house he would buy for them one day and the gifts he would lavish on his parents and his three sisters. He fantasized about whisking his family to Palm Beach in a private jet and putting them up at The Breakers, the most prestigious hotel there. He said to himself over and over, like a mantra, "I'll never be poor. I'll never have to struggle like my parents did."

Jeff's parents, extremely affectionate and caring, constantly let him know how much they loved him and how wonderful they thought he was. To his eventual misfortune, they were *not* particularly good at critiquing his behavior when appropriate. In addition to emotional nurturing, children need constructive criticism, so that they can learn how to do things properly instead of just avoiding, faking, or bungling them.

Because Jeff's parents had trouble making a success of their own lives, they didn't consider themselves equipped to teach their son very much about how to "make it" in the real world. Furthermore, they felt guilty for not giving him as much as they felt he deserved. Thus, instead of teaching him more effective ways of managing his life, they took the laissez-faire approach, leaving him to figure things out for himself.

Throughout his childhood, Jeff learned, "If I wait long enough, the problem will take care of itself." With three adoring older sisters and a doting mother, it wasn't difficult for him to let many things go—cleaning his room, returning his overdue books to the library, researching his school report—because one of them would invariably step in and do it for him. He didn't consciously plan for this; he just developed an unconscious habit of waiting, not doing things as they came along, and avoiding whatever was difficult as long as he could. He followed the same habit in other matters. If something turned out okay after all, despite his procrastination, he took the general credit for "managing things" well; if something didn't, he attributed it to bad luck.

When Jeff was sixteen, he had his first "official" job, working part time at a fast-food restaurant. But he felt humiliated working there and wished he could just hang out after school with the kids from more affluent families. Most of his time on the job was spent dreaming, and the manager—at first very pleased with his friendliness and competence—eventually fired him for "goofing off."

Jeff's teachers became similarly disillusioned with their "enchanted prince." His eleventh-grade adviser, summarizing teachers' opinions, told Jeff's mother, "Your son seems to spend most of his time in another world. He's not a problem kid or a poor performer. People like him, and as you know, his grades are good. It's just that he doesn't work up to his potential."

In college, Jeff followed the same basic pattern. He was often late with his homework assignments, and occasionally he wouldn't do them at all, but he always got by. Sometimes he'd nonchalantly take a failing grade for the work he hadn't done, knowing that his good grades in the course would ensure an acceptable final average. It didn't disturb him much that he wasn't *actually* achieving what he was *capable* of achieving. He relied on his self-inflating fantasies to make up the difference—both in his own mind and in the minds of people he wanted to impress.

Changing the Pattern

As a lifelong dreamer, Jeff practiced evasion as his immediate reaction to any new, sharp-edged reality, retreating into his comfortably cushioned self-made universe, where everything was vague and non-threatening. Here he felt entitled to clothe the naked truth, thereby rendering it more attractive. Indeed, he felt compelled to dress it up as much as he could. After all, that was both his special talent and his survival mechanism. This reflexive pattern repeatedly prevented him from confronting his real-life problems in any constructive way.

For example, shortly before Jeff came to me, he was forced to face the truth that he was almost bankrupt as the result of his extravagant $50,000 spending spree after he landed the design firm job. As I mentioned earlier, he was genuinely contrite, promising his wife and himself that he would start right away to pay off his debts and be more thrifty. Having made those promises, he suddenly had the germ of a new, more positive self-image—and he retreated to his dream world to feed it into a fantasy of a supermartyr. He took enormous pride in the fact that he signed a consolidated loan to pay off his credit card debt—too much pride, considering that the loan was mainly negotiated by his wife. He also couldn't help mentally puffing up the significance of every small sacrifice he made: buying the $150 pair of shoes instead of the $200 pair, skipping appetizers and desserts when he ate out, washing his car himself instead of using the drive-through service, denying himself a vacation in Mexico that was completely out of the question anyway.

Jeff the supermartyr couldn't see that he wasn't going far enough to make the *real* changes that were necessary. His poor financial situation cried out for him to take a full, businesslike inventory of his expenses and then make up a budget. Instead, he was arbitrarily "cutting down" here and there, an ill-defined, halfhearted strategy that was destined not to last for long. And while he needed to rescale his life so that he could live enjoyably *within* his means (for example, by vacationing at a local state park instead of going to Mexico), he was merely biding time (not vacationing at all) until he could once again get away with living *beyond* his means.

Knowing how entrenched Jeff's pattern of "reform-escapism" was, I recommended that he give himself as little room for escape as possible. I created a self-help program—"STAR"—that he could follow in everything he thought, said, and did:

      S - turning the vague into the *s*pecific
      T - turning the imaginative into the *t*ruthful
      A - turning the passive into the *a*ctive
      R - turning the romantic into the *r*ealistic

For example, it was apparent to me that Jeff, like most dreamer procrastinators, had trouble with the "middle" phase of a project. He was great at the initial conception, when he had more or less free rein to dream of what might be; and he could be equally good at the end of a project, knowing how to wrap things up and, of course, celebrate them and capitalize on them. The problem was that he often never got to the end of a project, because he couldn't get through the middle part, where the less dramatic, step-by-step task work lay. The middle phase of a project is crucial . . . *BUT* for the dreamer-procrastinator, it's too difficult, or boring, or tedious.

To help Jeff get through the middle part of his current project, job hunting, I recommended that he literally map it out in a special notebook that included calendar pages. First, he had to draw up a list of specific tasks that needed to get done (preparing his résumé, drafting a generic cover letter, sharpening his interview skills, researching trade periodicals, developing a phone list of people who could be helpful, making the phone calls, and so on); and then he had to put a deadline for each task on a time line. This effort gave Jeff's job hunt far more momentum —and more leads—over the next six weeks than he'd had during the previous three months.

Another particularly successful strategy in Jeff's "STAR" program involved his campaign to make more active use of his leisure time. He had always dreamed about excelling in the martial arts, so I urged him to turn this dream into a reality. Thereafter, for two hours every Saturday afternoon, instead of watching TV or reading espionage thrillers, he took a class in aikido, a Japanese martial art, which, though fluid and graceful, involves very robust turning, rolling, falling, and sparring with a short staff and a wooden sword. Besides getting him to go out and *do* something, it developed his skills of *committing* (attending the weekly class) and of *concentrating* (focusing closely on his own movements in relationship to those of his opponent).

If you're a dreamer procrastinator, it's high time for you to devise your own self-help program. If Jeff could do it, you can too!

HOW TO STOP BEING A DREAMER PROCRASTINATOR

If you scored high on the "dreamer" part of the quiz in Chapter 1, you probably caught glimpses of yourself as you read Jeff's story. Now you need a fuller self-portrait, in order to appreciate the specific nature of your personal procrastination problem and, ultimately, the specific ways in which you can help yourself to overcome it. Here's a self-assessment exercise to get you started:

1. Recall at least two different occasions when you were faced with a project and *had great fantasies about doing it . . . BUT never got it done.* For each occasion, ask yourself these questions:
   - What, specifically, was the stumbling block—in other words, what actually kept me from getting it done?
   - What were the consequences of not getting it done? How

did I feel? What effect did it have on my life? On my relationships?

2. Recall at least two different times when you *finished projects* . . . *BUT wasted time or got them done late* because you spent too much time dreaming instead of doing. For each occasion, ask yourself:
   • What, specifically, was I dreaming *about*?
   • What were the consequences of wasting time or being late? How did I feel? What effect did it have on my life? On my relationships?

Now that you've begun recalling more specific details about the part of you that's a dreamer procrastinator, you're ready to practice the strategies that work best to reeducate this aspect of yourself. When you have done so, your capacity to dream can become more helpful and less hurtful to yourself and to those around you. In your self-help program, be sure to give balanced attention to all three guideline categories: thinking, speaking, and acting.

CHANGING HOW YOU THINK

1. *Practice creative visualization.*

Being a dreamer procrastinator, you already spend too much time living in your head, so it may seem counterproductive for you to take on yet another creative mental activity. Nevertheless, it's essential to attack the problem at its source. Only by learning to improve the *way* in which you fantasize can you truly start transforming your dreams into realities.

The following creative visualization exercise involves

suspending all your normal, free-flowing fantasies and, instead, engaging in a specific *process* of imagination—one that allows you to experience in your mind what it's like to turn something abstract into something concrete, step by step. You can practice this visualization whenever you're stressed out or in need of motivation.

To try it now, first read it all the way through twice, or until you feel you know it fairly well. There's no need to memorize it word for word, as long as you can recall the major events. Then, when you feel ready to proceed, assume a comfortable position somewhere that's quiet, dimly lit, and free from distractions. Some people prefer lying on their back on the floor; others prefer sitting in a comfortable chair or couch.

After you've settled into your position, silently speak the guidelines to yourself, as you remember them. Go through the entire visualization scenario at a slow, relaxed pace, allowing at least a minute of quiet time between instructions. The entire exercise is designed to take between fifteen and twenty minutes.

If desired, you can record the guidelines word for word on an audiotape that you can replay whenever you want to repeat the imagery. As you record the guidelines, speak in a slow, soothing voice and allow a minute of silence between instructions. As an alternative to an audiotape, you can have a trusted family member or friend read the guidelines aloud while you visualize in response. If you choose this option, be sure to rehearse the reading before beginning.

Visualization for the Dreamer Procrastinator

(1) Close your eyes and take a few deep breaths to relax your body—inhaling slowly through your nose, then exhaling

slowly through your mouth. Let go of any tension or tight-ness in your body. Allow the thoughts and cares of the day to drift away, leaving your body light, your mind empty.

(2) In this relaxed state, picture yourself standing on the lawn of a park, holding the strings to three helium balloons: a red balloon, a yellow balloon, and a green balloon. You look up and admire the three colored balloons, swaying in the blueness of the clear, sunlit sky.

(3) Now look more closely at each balloon and imagine you see a dark, vague shape inside it. You can't quite make out what any of these three shapes are, no matter how long or carefully you look at them.

(4) Still noticing the dark shapes inside each of the three colored balloons, imagine you see the balloons bumping into each other and feel them tugging on their strings. Imagine these motions gradually increasing in intensity until it becomes awkward and uncomfortable to keep holding the strings.

(5) Now picture a pole set in the ground next to you, about waist high, with a hook at the top. You tie all the balloon strings to this pole.

(6) Imagine grabbing hold of the string to the red balloon. You pull this balloon down to the ground on your left, and burst it with a pin. There, amid the red balloon fragments, you see a flat square of wood. You realize it is the floor to a miniature house, and you place it on the ground to the right of you.

(7) Now, grabbing hold of the string to the yellow balloon, you pull this balloon down to the ground on your left, and burst it with a pin. There, amid the yellow balloon

fragments, you see four smaller squares of wood. You realize these four pieces are the walls to the house. You turn to your right and fit each wall piece into a groove on the floor piece, until all the walls are in place.

(8) Finally, grabbing hold of the string to the green balloon, you pull this balloon down to the ground on your left, and burst it with a pin. There, amid the green balloon fragments, you see a small wood roof. Taking it into your hand, you turn to your right and place it on top of the four walls of the house.

(9) Now step back and admire the miniature house that you've built. You see it slowly growing, until it is a beautiful full-size house. You go inside and see one comfortable chair in the center of the floor. You sink into this chair and relax. When you're completely relaxed, you hear a voice within you saying, "You have done a good job. When you take matters into your own hands and work hard on them, you can build great things."

(10) Savoring these words and appreciating a job well done, you continue to sit in this relaxed state. Notice how good it feels to rest with a sense of accomplishment. Take as much time as you need, and whenever you are ready, slowly open your eyes. With your eyes fully open, say something positive about your ability to make things happen, and believe it with all your heart.

2. *Be mindful of the difference between "feeling good" and "feeling good about yourself."*

As a dreamer procrastinator, you need to guard against your proclivity to seek pleasure from being passive—just letting time, and goal-related pressures, drift on by as you watch TV, read a lightweight novel, or lounge in the sun like a lizard on a rock. There's nothing wrong with relaxing from time to time; but when you're predisposed to doing it too much, it's at the expense of your self-esteem and well-being.

Feeling good *about yourself,* as opposed to simply feeling good, has to do with taking pride in accomplishment. On a short-term basis, you may not feel good pushing yourself to jog farther than you ever have before, or to get ahead on a complicated work project, or to earn an "A" grade rather than a "B." However, on a long-term basis, the self-confidence and self-respect you will acquire from performing these activities will make you feel deeply and enduringly good about just being yourself. You will come to enjoy living a more active life of "doing," which will make you less emotionally dependent on withdrawing from life.

3. *Avoid indulging a "private" self-image that's at odds with your "public" image.*

Stop yourself when you begin to engage in self-stroking reveries of being more important, successful, talented, or interesting than other people realize. This type of passive fantasizing can easily wind up taking the place of actually doing things that demonstrate your worthiness or special-ness to other people—as well as to yourself.

There are many insidious ways that you can go about creating troublesome conflicts between your private self-image and your public image, and you have to remain alert to spot them. You may catch yourself "reinventing" real-life experiences in your head—for example, a long-ago athletic competition or a recent fight with a colleague—so that you play a more flattering role. Or you may find that you habitually act one way (appropriate to your "inner" self) but say or do something entirely different (appropriate to your "outer" self). These inconsistencies work to undermine your sense of identity and increase your tendency to exaggerate your accomplishments.

4. *Train yourself to differentiate between dreams and goals.*

Dreams are always very loose-knit in structure. Sometimes they are nothing more than gossamer images of what we desire: a trophy, a mansion, a check for one million dollars, a certain face gazing at us adoringly, a deserted beach on a tropical island. Other times, they may have all the richness and scope of a motion picture, but they're still fragmentary. We may dream, for example, of rising to the top of our profession, with many detailed scenes of the miracles we accomplish, the recognition we receive, and the thrills we savor; but inevitably, there are key scenes missing—the non-glamorous, step-by-step tasks we performed on our way toward accomplishing those miracles, receiving that recognition, and savoring those thrills.

A goal, in contrast to a dream, is a more tightly knit enterprise. It involves a *specific* objective, which is to be achieved by taking *specific* steps over a *specific* period of time. A dream remains un-doable until it is translated into a goal, and this is what you should strive for with any and every dream that you take seriously.

Let's assume, for example, that you have a dream image of being on a tropical beach. You can turn that into a goal by saying to yourself, "I'm taking a vacation in Jamaica for ten days in February." Having this goal, you can begin right away to develop the action steps that will get you there: consulting with a travel agent, setting up a budget to save the money, and so on. Your goal gives you a clear end point, and a means of measuring your progress toward that end point.

Assuming that you have a much larger dream—e.g., to

go to the top of your profession—you can still apply the same translating process, saying to yourself, for example, "I'm going to become the president of my own company within six years." Then you can start planning the necessary action steps. If those steps appear too ambitious—or easier than you imagined—then the goal can be amended with a more realistic but equally specific time frame. The important point is to be specific: Dreams aren't, but goals have to be!

5. *Develop the habit of thinking with "5 W's and 1 H."*
   To ground your thinking, practice subjecting your vague fantasies and ideas to "5 W's and 1 H": *w*hat, *w*hen, *w*here, *w*ho, *w*hy, and *h*ow. Here's a model to get you started, based on the idea "I want to be rich."
   • *What* do I realistically think I can earn?
   • *When* will I be able to earn that?
   • *Where* could I work that would enable me to do that?
   • *Who* would hire or help me?
   • *Why* do I want to be rich?
   • *How* can I earn what I would like to earn?
   There are two good reasons to perform this exercise. First, it leads you to develop an idea into a firm, step-by-step action plan. Second, it gets you to examine an idea from multiple perspectives, so that it can start taking on more realistic dimensions.

CHANGING HOW YOU SPEAK

1. *Change your "wish"es, "like to"s, and "try to"s to "will"s.*
   Listen more closely to the way you talk about your future. As a dreamer procrastinator, you'll discover that you use a

lot of tentative, non-committing verbs: "I *wish* I could think of a solution"; "I'd *like to* go hiking in the mountains this spring"; "I'll *try to* do the job well."

As an exercise in getting yourself to speak more assertively and, therefore, to make more of a commitment toward taking action, practice substituting "I *will*" for "I *wish*," "I'd *like to*" or "I'll *try to*." For example, instead of saying, "I *wish* I could" (or "I'd *like to*" or "I'll *try to*") "lose ten pounds," say, "I *will* lose ten pounds." This more definite form of expression encourages you to take one step further by articulating what you're actually going to do—e.g., "I will lose ten pounds by following the Fat-B-Gone weight-loss program."

The phrase "*try to*" can be especially problematic for dreamer procrastinators, who are inclined to back away from actually *doing* things. The notion of *trying* to do something holds within it the self-defeating possibility of failure. For example, hearing an airline ticket officer say, "I'll try my best" is never as encouraging as hearing the officer say, "I'll do my best."

Granted, there are some things that may be ultimately out of your control, so that you can only *try to* control them—e.g., "I'm going to try to get a promotion." However, many things are well within your control, and as a result, you can do much better than simply *try to* control them. For example, it's more appropriate and effective to say, "I *will* write a letter to my mother tonight" than "I will *try to* write a letter to my mother tonight."

When I'm consulting with dreamer-procrastinator patients who overuse the phrase "try to," I often throw a pillow on the floor and ask them to "try to" pick it up. Inevitably, they're confused by my request. "What do you mean, 'try to'?" they'll say. "How do you 'try to' pick a pillow up? You either do it or you don't." And then they get the point: It's a case of either picking it up or not picking it up. The concept of "trying to" pick it up is a bogus one.

2. *Change your "someday"s and "soon"s to specific times.*

   "Any day now" has a habit of never coming. In fact, it is no specific day at all. In referring to *when* you are going to do something, be as specific as possible, so that you don't give yourself an excuse to let matters drift. Instead of saying, "I'll clean that closet *someday*," say, "I'll clean that closet *next Saturday afternoon.*" Instead of saying, "I'll be done with that report soon," say, "I'll be done with that report *by February 1*" (or "*by 3 P.M.*").

3. *Replace vague, passive language with concrete, active language.*

   As you continue to listen to yourself talk, you'll become aware of more and more subtle ways in which you speak evasively or unclearly—the preferred language style of the dreamer procrastinator. For example, in order to obscure your personal responsibility, you might find yourself saying to someone, "I have a cash flow problem," instead of "I'm in debt"; or "It's a lazy day today," instead of "I feel lazy." Or, in order to take one, self-deluding step back from admitting the truth, you might find yourself using vague qualifying phrases in your speech, like "I'm *getting* out of shape," instead of "I *am* out of shape."

   Practice avoiding this euphemistic, overqualified way of speaking. Get in the habit of stating facts as clearly, concisely, and directly as you can, so that there's no room for dreamlike confusion on either your own or someone else's part. At first, you may feel uncomfortable speaking in this uncharacteristically direct manner; but as you keep practicing, it will come to you more naturally, and you will experience a greater sense of having genuinely communicated with others.

4. *Avoid engaging in "make-believe" talk.*

Finally, you need to guard against using the kind of magical, "say it and it's true" language that's dearest to the heart of the dreamer procrastinator—what I call "make-believe" talk. Here are some examples:

- "I deserve more than I'm getting."
- "I'm entitled to take some time off."
- "I know it will all come out okay in the end."
- "I'm the best person they ever had in this job."
- "I shouldn't have to account for my time."

This kind of language usually reflects wishful thinking rather than reality. On occasion, there *may* be *some* truth behind what's being said, but that truth is not specifically expressed: It would ruin the grandiose effect!

When you find yourself tempted to make such self-inflating statements, allow yourself one of two options: either don't make the statement at all or back it up with facts—in which case your original statement may need to be rendered less extreme. For example, instead of saying, "I deserve more than I'm getting," say either nothing at all or something that can be substantiated, like, "I deserve a raise because I've brought in more sales volume the past quarter than any of my colleagues." Or instead of saying, "I'm the best person they ever had in this job," say either nothing at all or something like, "My success in raising student scores over a year's time has been greater than that of my last three predecessors." And be sure that your "facts" are true—not just pompous boasting.

CHANGING HOW YOU ACT

1. *Plan each major project in writing, using a time line.*

By literally outlining on paper the specific milestones and deadlines involved in completing a project, you help make yourself more responsible—and better equipped—to get them done. You also give yourself an instrument with which you can measure your progress along the way, thus improving your ability to cope with unexpected difficulties that might otherwise serve as excuses to give up.

On the top of a sheet of paper, write down the goal you want to achieve and the date by which you want to achieve it. Be as specific as possible: "Redoing the den by this winter" is *not* nearly as helpful as "Having a den with freshly painted walls, built-in bookcases, a new couch, and a better phone-fax system by December 1."

Then, on the left-hand side of the sheet, draw a vertical line from top to bottom. This is the time line for the project. Put today's date next to a mark at the top of the line, and the final-goal date next to a mark at the bottom. In the above example, the final-goal date is December 1.

Next, on a separate piece of paper, list the major tasks that need to be done to reach the goal. In the above example, the tasks might be: painting the walls, building the bookcases, purchasing a new couch, buying a better phone-fax system.

Finally, figure out logical time frames and sequences for doing these tasks and enter each task-plus-deadline at an appropriate point on the time line of your original goal sheet. You may find it helpful to break down major tasks into minor tasks and put deadlines for these minor tasks on the time line as well. For example, "painting the walls" could be broken down into "choosing paint color(s)," "buying paint and materials," and "painting walls," each with its own deadline.

2. *Buy and maintain two huge calendars: one for your job and one for your home/personal life.*

Put each calendar in a highly visible, easily accessible place. Mark each with important milestones, deadlines, and events (see the discussion of "time lines," above) as soon as they are known. Refer to both of them *at least* twice each day—at the beginning and at the end—and be sure to mark off each milestone, deadline, or event as it's completed.

3. *Keep two lists with you as you go about each day: a "to do" and a "to think about" list.*

On your "to do" list, write tasks that you're definitely committed to doing that day (for starters, consult your two calendars). Express each task in an action-oriented way, with as many specific references as possible—e.g., "buying a gift for Mary's birthday during lunch hour," instead of "gift for Mary."

On your "to think about" list, write tasks that you're considering doing today, or in the near future, but that need more pondering. Express such tasks as specifically as possible, making clear what requires further thought—e.g., "determining three future improvements to discuss at next week's staff meeting" instead of "prepare for staff meeting."

Preestablish routine times for the following three list-related activities:

- making the two lists (e.g., either the night before or first thing in the morning)
- checking them during the day (e.g., at noon)

• reviewing them afterward (e.g., at 5 P.M. or just before retiring)

In addition, cross off each item *when completed*—it will help bolster your sense of accomplishment.

The purpose of keeping these two separate lists, instead of one composite list, is to train yourself to distinguish between things that you're definitely committed to doing and things that you may or may not do, depending upon your time, energy, and/or further thoughts. Dreamer procrastinators tend to let most things drift into the latter category, whether or not it's appropriate!

4. *Each day, assign yourself at least one special "to do" task in addition to several ordinary ones.*

"Ordinary tasks" are essentially maintenance tasks that you need to do in order to preserve the status quo: "get a haircut," "fill out time sheets," "return calls," "pick up dry cleaning." By contrast, "special tasks" are venture activities—ones that are aimed toward moving you ahead in life: "talk with newsletter editor about submitting an article," "pick up travel brochures for possible summer vacation," "visit design center to get new product ideas."

As a dreamer procrastinator, you need to make a concerted effort to accomplish all of your ordinary tasks, so it's best not to let a day go by without doing at least a few. At the same time, scheduling at least one "special" task each day will help you to learn how to bring your dreams into reality.

5. *Use an alarm, a timer, or a beeper as a reminder to do a task.*

It may go against your dreamer nature to rely on mechanical aids to spur you to action, but they can be surprisingly effective. For example, assuming you're serious about wanting to complete a project by 4 P.M., why not set a watch to beep at that time (or even an hour ahead), to make sure you don't lose track of the deadline—something that dreamer procrastinators are highly likely to do?

Experiment with different kinds of alarms, timers, or beepers to find the most convenient one(s) for your needs. You might also consider asking another person to be your reminder on certain specific occasions, as long as it isn't too burdensome for them. Just be careful not to overuse other people as reminders, or you may never learn to assume that responsibility for yourself.

6. *Do fewer passive activities and more active ones.*

Instead of passively lounging in bed, watching TV, or reading, try being more active, so that you'll condition yourself to *do* instead of simply to *think.* Some dreamer procrastinators find it helpful to look each day for active things they can do with their *hands,* their *mouth,* and their *feet.* For example:

> *Hands:* write a letter, organize a file, paint a cabinet
> *Mouth:* telephone a friend, ask a task-oriented question, talk to the neighbor about gardening
> *Feet:* walk to the store instead of driving, jog as you walk the dog, dance to the music you're listening to

7. *Seek more interaction with other people.*

Nothing works better to keep you from losing yourself in your dreams than becoming more involved with other people. Aside from the fresh, "real-life" perspectives, ideas, and motivational pushes that other people can give you, there's the issue of protecting yourself from your own insularity. You could be fooling yourself far more than you realize about what's true or false, harmful or helpful, possible or impossible, difficult or easy.

Make sure that your dialogues with other people are truly interactive. Instead of doing all the talking, or keeping the conversation focused totally on yourself, make a special effort to listen attentively to other people, to ask them questions about their experiences, thoughts, and feelings. Seek out others' viewpoints, obtaining input from them regarding your projects. Hearing their ideas can be much more productive than simply bragging or tooting your own horn.

Chapter 4

The Worrier
Procrastinator

*". . . But I'm afraid to make
a change!"*

Who among us does not worry about the future from time to time—wondering whether a certain project or event will turn out okay, fearing to make a mistake, conjuring up "what if" catastrophes? We all do, and every act of procrastination—regardless of who commits it—involves a certain amount of this kind of concern. Some people, however, are unusually apprehensive by nature and, as a result, more inclined than the average person to avoid or delay doing things. I call these people "worrier procrastinators."

Compared to other people, worrier procrastinators have a small and sharply defined "comfort zone." They feel safe with familiar, predictable, and therefore dependable routines, and very insecure with any new challenge that is unpredictable and, therefore, potentially upsetting. This response applies not only to major life issues, such as changing to a better job or pursuing a promising relationship, but also to minor, day-to-day issues, like starting a new work assignment or going out for the evening. Worrier procrastinators are so alert to the negative possibilities of an unknown situation, and so blind to the positive ones, that they tend to freeze where they are—inside their own comfort zone—instead of moving forward into a future that lies beyond their range of vision.

In many cases, a worrier procrastinator is all too keenly aware

of his or her hyperanxiety. It springs to the surface the moment
the status quo is threatened. Patti, a forty-three-year-old homemaker and part-time receptionist, complains:

> I dread facing decisions. As soon as I do, I start to obsess about
> what might go wrong. This spring, my husband and I were plan-
> ning to go to North Carolina to visit my son and daughter-in-
> law. I should have been excited about it, but I couldn't let go
> of my fears: What if a whole week is too long for them, or for
> us? What if they're really busy then? What if the weather's
> horrible? What if we have car trouble? In the end, I waited too
> long to make arrangements, and we never did go. My husband
> says he's going to drag me there this fall, come hell or high
> water!

Patti's chronic uneasiness seeps into every area of her life,
causing her to delay, forgo, or complicate all sorts of endeavors
that might bring her pleasure or self-advancement. For safety's
sake, she's spent six years being a part-time receptionist rather
than taking the scary plunge into full-time administrative work
that a part of her has always longed to take. She and her husband
are good friends with another couple who are constantly inviting
them to sail on their boat, but Patti hasn't yet accepted. Not
having a clear picture of what a sailing outing might be like, her
hesitant "I don't know"s always devolve into nos.

Stan, a forty-year-old claims manager in a large, well-
established insurance firm, is a different kind of worrier procrastinator. He's not quite as conscious of his procrastination
problem as Patti is. Instead, he considers himself simply stable
and prudent. "I made a choice a long time ago to avoid anything
that's too difficult or too much work," he tells people. "I guess
I'm basically a lazy, low-energy person."

Stan may think of himself as a "lazy, low-energy person," but
underneath the composed surface is a nervous man who suffers

a great deal of angst in coming to a decision. He's especially reluctant to make the types of judgment calls that are often involved in insurance claims. Therefore, he chronically procrastinates with his work.

Stan assumes his ex-wife divorced him because he was, in his words, "too dull," but actually she left him because he was, in her words, "constantly exhausting himself, and me, with all his worrying." As their marriage dragged on, his wife felt compelled against her will to assume more and more of the decision-making responsibility. He continued not only to dodge decision-making but also to withhold his emotions and constrict his ambitions. Too much time went by with too little progress on his part toward achieving the dreams he and his wife had when they married. Now he's alone and, thanks to his safety-conscious inertia, likely to stay that way for some time.

Such are the troubles that worrier procrastinators create for themselves, whether they're aware of it or not. In addition to their overall fearfulness, worrier procrastinators display the following four characteristics:

1. *Lacking confidence in their own abilities, worrier procrastinators tend to avoid or delay doing things.*

   Worrier procrastinators suffer from low self-esteem. Assuming they will be incapable of managing any trouble they might encounter in a new project, they often avoid it altogether, or else put off doing it as long as they can. Patti, for example, resists getting a much-coveted administrative job because she fears that she might not be skillful enough to handle it.

   If and when worrier procrastinators do finally start a project, they either proceed very slowly and cautiously or take as many breaks as they can, resulting in a waste of time and energy. This is the way Stan handles his work-related tasks. He disparages himself as being lazy, but his primary problem is worrier procrastination.

2. *Worrier procrastinators are indecisive in general and often fail to commit themselves to the specific decisions they do make.*

    Worrier procrastinators have difficulty committing themselves wholeheartedly to a decision. Instead, they offer a tentative commitment at best and keep themselves ever on guard to hold back or withdraw if things don't go smoothly.

    Patti, for example, sincerely wanted to go visit her son and daughter-in-law in the spring, but she felt that she couldn't make any firm decision about the trip until she could convince herself it wouldn't present any problems. She thereby put herself into an impossible, "no-win" situation. Nobody can control the future; all one can do is trust in oneself to make the most of what the future brings.

    Stan is indecisive in the same way. He depends upon his highly structured job to make decisions for him, just as he once relied on his more decisive wife to do so. Instead of driving himself through life by his own effort and skill, he just coasts along in neutral, hoping to avoid problems, unaware of the difficulties his indecisiveness creates.

3. *Worrier procrastinators are excessively dependent upon others for advice, reassurance, nurturance, and help.*

    A combination of low self-esteem and indecisiveness compels worrier procrastinators to turn to other, more confident people for reassurance and direction. It's as if the former were helpless and scared children, and the latter their more competent parents, obligated to do for them.

    The truth is that one's friends, colleagues, and personal partners are *not* in one's life to function as parents—a truth that worrier procrastinators have trouble appreciating. They're in the habit of relying too much on the people who are close to them, either to help them through a troublesome situation or, even better, to take over responsibility for that situation. We see this in the way that Patti forces her husband to "drag" her to North Carolina, "come hell or high water," and in the way that Stan once depended on his wife to handle almost all of the decisions in their marital life.

4. *Preferring the safety of the "known" to the risk of the "unknown," worrier procrastinators have a high resistance to change.*

Like Dorothy in L. Frank Baum's *The Wizard of Oz*, worrier procrastinators can be quite fascinated by new people and new experiences—in their dreams. When confronted with them in reality, however, they head for home as quickly as they can. To them, anything that's not familiar is, above all, dangerous; and anything that's dangerous is to be bypassed.

The smallest things, if they entail an unknown element, can loom as potential ordeals to the worrier procrastinator. Cleaning the garage becomes "unthinkable"—and therefore "un-doable"—because it means facing immense messes and decision-making crises. The prospect of writing a letter stirs up discouraging images of not being able to express one's thoughts accurately or cleverly and therefore of being misunderstood or ridiculed. Even planning a day at the beach triggers fears of being trapped in beach-bound traffic, of getting sunburned, or of becoming bored with nothing to do but relax.

Patti exhibits her fear of change by refusing to leave the known safety of her undemanding job for a better, more demanding one. She can't even bring herself to leave the known safety of her home to visit her son and daughter-in-law! Stan feels the same "change phobia." He didn't allow his marriage to evolve; and now he won't allow himself to grow.

The price paid by worrier procrastinators is a steep one. Day by day, and year by year, they not only miss deadlines and due dates; they also miss opportunities and adventures. Consider the case of my client Joan.

JOAN: THE WORRIER PROCRASTINATOR

Joan first arrived at my office thirty minutes late and very apologetic. "I'm so sorry," she blurted out, before anything else was said. "I got lost coming here." She looked frightened and bewildered, like a child expecting to be punished—an image that was bolstered by her youthful face and casual attire (jeans and a T-shirt).

After I welcomed Joan and reassured her that everything was fine, she burst into a big smile, but it quickly vanished. As she settled into a chair, I again saw a pleading look on her face. "How shall I begin, Doctor?" she asked. Already she was depending upon me—to a greater degree than most first-time clients—for approval and direction: the first indications, I later realized, of her "worrier" personality.

During that initial meeting, Joan's main concern was her passivity. She admitted:

When I'm not actually working, I often lie around reading magazines and watching TV for hours on end. I've got other things that need to be done, but I just can't bring myself to do them. So I have my freedom, my nice-and-easy time, but then I have to pay this terrible price for it later, when I'm forced to do the mountain of work I've been putting off. Then I get disgusted with myself. I tell myself, "You're so stupid! How could you have sat around doing nothing for so long? What's the matter with you?"

In subsequent sessions, as we more closely examined her present and past experiences, Joan came to appreciate that her procrastination problem involved many other issues besides just physical "passivity." She also was seriously lacking in self-confidence, which made her excessively reliant on others for advice or support and, in some cases, for outright relief or rescue. "I feel as if I'm still not an adult yet but an overgrown kid," she told me once. "There are too many times I just don't know what to do and wish somebody would step in and take care of things for me."

Time after time, Joan hesitated to act in a more decisive, timely, or effective manner because of her fear that she would fail or wind up doing the "wrong thing." For this reason, she found it extremely difficult to commit herself to specific tasks or projects. "Ideally, I wouldn't have to make any decisions on my own," she declared. "I avoid assuming responsibility now as much as I can, even when I know I'm the one who should do it, or when no one else is around who could do it. I get panicky whenever I'm called upon to do something new."

Our mission together for the next few months was to explore precisely how Joan's tendency toward "worrier procrastination" manifested itself in her day-to-day life. Only then could we devise a specific plan for overcoming it on a day-to-day basis.

Procrastinating at Work

While Joan was at work, teaching her fourth grade class, her worrier-procrastination problems were not as evident as they were at other times. Like most elementary school teachers, she was obligated to structure each school day according to a pre-determined, officially sanctioned lesson plan designed to ensure instructional consistency among teachers at the same grade level. When she was not occupied in fulfilling these pre-set requirements, she was busy responding to the momentary needs of her individual students. In both situations, she functioned reasonably well by depending upon someone or something else to determine—and enforce—her course of action.

Occasionally, however, Joan did encounter a work-related challenge to which she responded in a classic worrier-procrastinator manner. For example, the previous year she had become involved in a PTA-based committee that was assigned to create a program of monthly after-school cultural activities for the students—a chamber music concert, a visit to the art museum, etc. As the representative of the teaching staff, she was assigned to contact local cultural organizations that might volunteer to present events for the program. Much to her own frustration, she had found herself paralyzed with fear that she would be unable to do this job successfully. As a result, she had made too few calls too late for a program to materialize during that particular year, and still she was doing nothing, hoping that the other committee members wouldn't bring it up again.

There was also now a larger source of concern relating to her job. She loved the children, and she was good at teaching them, but she felt as if she were in a rut, repeating the same thing year after year. Even though she still worked as hard in her seventh year of teaching as she had in her first—always reviewing her lessons carefully to guard against making mistakes—and even though she still received excellent evaluations, she no longer experienced the drive to teach, or the joy of teaching, that she'd known during the first few years.

Joan recognized that she was going through the "burnout"

syndrome, a common, much-discussed phenomenon in the teaching profession. She also knew that there are many different approaches toward dealing with it effectively, but she preferred to turn a deaf ear to all of them. It was less frightening to continue doing what she already knew how to do than to try something different, whether it be a new way of teaching, a new teaching assignment, or another, more personally fulfilling career altogether. Nevertheless, she couldn't help worrying that she'd turn out like some of her colleagues ten or twenty years older than herself who were totally burned out and desperate to retire.

Procrastination on a Personal Level

I once asked Joan to describe herself in a single short sentence, and she replied, with a strong hint of self-disparagement, "I believe in safety first." And yet, a few moments later, she told me that she loved novels and movies in which the heroine takes great risks: with courageous stands, adventurous exploits, or dangerous men. She said she thought of these women as "hardy and resourceful" and wished she could be that way. Although she was often commended by colleagues for her ability to manage a tight classroom and keep her equilibrium during faculty squabbles, she knew deep down that it had more to do with a reactive fear of trouble than a decisive self-reliance.

Without work routines to keep her going at a reasonably steady pace, Joan would, in her words, "hole up like a mole." It was an appropriate image for her style of procrastination: one in which inactivity and self-created "blindness" provide a form of de facto protection from the scary uncertainties of the world. To avoid facing—and, ultimately, doing something about—her unsatisfying social life, her outgrown apartment, or her dreams of accomplishing something important, she burrowed into her favorite, overstuffed chair in the living room and lost herself in reading and watching TV.

Joan's worrier procrastination also revealed itself in the way she went about handling small, daily tasks. She considered herself too burdened with her troubles to bother being properly attentive to chores, and so they grew in number and complexity, until they, too, became onerous to think about—much less to perform. She told me, "I have this ongoing fantasy about having a personal servant who follows me around and does all the things I hate doing, like cleaning the oven or writing thank-you notes."

In describing these relatively trivial and routine tasks, Joan unwittingly transformed them into intimidating feats that she felt somehow compelled to avoid. Even going to bed at night became an exercise in dodging any dreaded discomfort, as one of her "confessions" made clear:

> I take off my clothes at night and I just drop them on the floor. I leave a trail with my shoes, slacks, blouse. I just can't wait to get into bed. I know everything will be wrinkled, but my need to be cozy in bed overrides this knowledge. It sounds as if I'm being lazy, but to me, it feels more as if I'm fleeing something scary and snuggling into something safe.

Joan's worrier procrastination also adversely affected her romantic relationships. Time after time, she had become too quickly involved with an inappropriate man simply so that she wouldn't have to be alone. Always wanting to have *someone* around to do things for her and to give her a sense of safety, she would never take upon herself the task of ending the relationship, even when it became clear that it was not working out.

Thus, again and again, Joan had kept herself tied for too long to an emotionally overbearing or undermining oaf—a far, dispiriting cry from the knight in shining armor whom she secretly craved. Each time, her extended, self-imposed entrapment only reinforced her lack of self-confidence, until, finally, the oaf would lumber away on his own. Once more, she would be the rejected partner, worried about her attractiveness and value to *any* man, let alone one who was more worthwhile.

By the time Joan came to me for therapy, she had suffered so much hurt from failed love affairs that—despite her dislike of being alone—she was afraid to commit to any relationship and rarely dated. "I still want someone to take care of me," she told me, "but I panic at the thought of letting someone get close. I'm too afraid that they'll find me wanting, then abandon me or throw me out."

How It All Got Started

Joan's worrier procrastination problems could be easily traced to her childhood. Her father, an accountant, was a strong-willed, emotionally distant, and meticulous man who had little to do with the actual tasks of raising his daughter. Nevertheless, his high standards and extreme attention to detail had an ever-present and distressing impact on Joan. She told me:

> I was always on edge around my father, always fearful that I'd be called to account. And yet I couldn't break free of my dependence on him. I still find myself drawn to strong men, to controllers. Like my father, they expect more from me than I can give. They say I take advantage of them, wanting them to do too much.

Left to herself to manage most of the child-rearing responsibilities, and well aware of her husband's aloofness, Joan's mother was always around, doing whatever she could to make her daughter "feel good." This phrase became her mother's motto: "Are you sure you're feeling good about this, Joan?" "You must feel good about what you're doing." "Well, it's okay with me, as long as it makes you feel good." Thus, the quick impulsive "fix" of *feeling* good began to take precedence in Joan's value system over planning, deciding, or committing to personal goals.

For most of her childhood, Joan's hesitation to act or think for herself had no major consequences, since her mother did a lot of her acting and thinking for her. If Joan was slow or loath to perform a certain task, like straightening her room, finishing a term report, or planning a Halloween costume, her mother would literally take it out of her hands and do it for her. Her mother enjoyed not only the work itself but also the sensation of being needed; in addition, her taking things over prevented any scenes about Joan's inefficiency, whether it be a confrontation between her and Joan or between Joan and her easily angered father.

During her school years, Joan was chronically slow to do her schoolwork; and when she finally did get around to doing it (providing her mother didn't do it for her), she put in as little time as she could to earn a decent mark. It wasn't that the schoolwork was intrinsically difficult; she just had an unusually strong aversion to doing anything that required more than minimal effort.

Instead of studying or developing new skills, Joan spent most of her time with her friends. She got along well with almost everyone, but she was usually a follower rather than a leader. "In high school, I refused to do anything that was dangerous or hard," she said, "but I loved hanging around people who did. I got a secret thrill out of hearing their stories of sneaking out at night or pulling some practical joke on a teacher."

Joan's tendency toward playing it safe and living within her comfort zone persisted throughout her teenage years. As a result, she never managed to develop a secure self-concept. "I still don't know who I really am," she complained to me. "I've never strayed from the straight and narrow; I've never climbed over the guardrails. I have no idea who I *could* be if I gave myself more freedom."

Whenever a friend asked Joan to try a potentially invigorating new experience, she'd initially get excited but then would quickly become so anxious that she'd back out. For example, when she was a junior in high school, she turned down an all-expense-paid skiing vacation to Colorado with her best friend's family because, she explained, "I can't ski, and I'm so clumsy I'm sure I'll hurt myself." In fact, Joan had no basis for claiming that she was clumsy by nature. If there were any truth to the matter, it was the other way around: She was so afraid of hurting herself that she might very well have made herself clumsy.

Just before Joan's second year in college, she and three other girls planned to rent an apartment close to the campus—a step that they all agreed would offer them a much better quality of life than dorm residence. Joan's mother was willing and even eager to pay most of the rent, just to make her daughter "feel good" about where she lived. But at the last minute, unable to deal with the turmoil of having three roommates and not knowing for sure what apartment life would be like, Joan changed her mind. She remained in the dorms—safe, secure, and bored— for the rest of college. Her first apartment came with her first teaching job; and she was still holding on to the same job and the same apartment seven years later, when she became my client.

Changing the Pattern

As the weeks passed and Joan revealed to me more and more of her frustrations, regrets, and inhibitions, there finally came a point when she cried out, "I'm so bored with my life that I'm sick of it!"

"Congratulations!" I replied. "Being sick of something can be a great motivator!"

And so it was for Joan. Eager to infuse her routine life with some new energy, Joan was primed and willing to take a risk. We settled on a limited risk for her first effort: taking up the after-school cultural project that she'd quietly dropped a few months earlier. She was still beating herself up over this instance of "worrier procrastination," so it seemed to be the perfect test issue. It wasn't a completely new challenge, but it was still a fresh one. And by making even a few steps toward managing it, she'd be greatly reducing the negative impact it had already had on her self-esteem.

Among the first things Joan tried to do was to change the way she talked about the project. For example, on several former occasions, when explaining to me why she had been afraid to make calls to the local symphony orchestra, she had said, "I don't know anything about classical music." I suggested that she stop making simple "I don't know" statements and, instead, make more positive compound statements, using this format: "I don't know . . . but one thing I *do* know is . . ." By experimenting with this technique, Joan developed a number of self-motivating leads on how to proceed with the project:

> I don't know anything about classical music, but one thing I *do* know is that I'm not a stupid person and that I can ask good questions.

> I don't know anything about classical music, but one thing I *do* know is what the school can and can't offer for a visiting ensemble.

> I don't know anything about classical music, but one thing I *do* know is that I need to have a talk with the symphony office before I can go any further with this school-related project.

> I don't know anything about classical music, but one thing I *do* know is where to look, whom to ask, and what to do to acquire more knowledge.

Another, more active strategy Joan employed to get herself moving on the cultural events project was to create a time line for it. She literally drew a vertical line on a piece of paper, with the current date at one end and, at the other end, the date by which she wanted the project finished. Then, all along this line, she noted important milestones—among them, the individual dates by which she needed to talk to individual organizations, arrange a tentative schedule, and make final bookings.

Having this time line to follow removed a considerable amount of Joan's anxiety. At a single glance, she could see that the project was not as complicated as she had originally feared, if she just took it one step at a time.

Joan was still "living by the rules," but now she was helping to formulate those rules instead of merely following the rules that others made for her. You can learn to do the same!

HOW TO STOP BEING A WORRIER PROCRASTINATOR

Before you do anything else, you need to refine your awareness of the specific ways in which you tend to be a worrier procrastinator. Keeping some specific images in your mind of what you *don't* want to happen, based on past problems, will help you to achieve what you *do* want to happen in the future. Use this self-assessment exercise as a starting point:

1. Recall at least two different occasions when you were faced with *something you wanted or needed to do BUT never did* because you were afraid. For each occasion, ask yourself these questions:
   • What, specifically, was I afraid of?
   • What were the consequences of my not doing it? How

did I feel? What effect(s) did it have on my life? On my relationships?

2. Recall at least two different occasions when you *finished a project BUT wasted time or got it done late* because of excessive fears or worries. For each occasion, ask yourself these questions:
   • What, specifically, were my fears and worries?
   • What were the consequences of wasting time or being late? How did I feel? What effects(s) did it have on my life? On my relationships?

From this starting point, you can go on to think of additional times when you let fears and worries sabotage your happiness. You can also begin overcoming your tendencies toward worrier procrastination by applying the following guidelines to your thinking, speaking, and acting. Be sure to give an appropriate amount of attention to each of these three categories!

CHANGING HOW YOU THINK

1. *Practice creative visualization.*

The best way to combat mental fear is to develop a counteractive frame of mind: one that is positive, confident, and easy to shift into whenever you feel your anxiety level rising. Wanting to help my worrier-procrastinator clients in this endeavor, I developed the following "anti-worry" visualization. Besides using it to overcome specific procrastination crises, practice it on a regular basis (say, twice a week), so that you can deepen your skill in performing it.

Before trying it now, read it slowly two times, or until you feel you know it fairly well. Word-for-word memorization is not necessary, provided you can re-create in your own words the same basic sequence of events. When you feel ready to begin, assume a comfortable position lying down on the floor or sitting on a chair or couch. Then silently review the guidelines to yourself, as you remember them, at a slow, relaxed pace. Be sure to allow about a minute of silence between instructions to dwell on the particular visual image that you've just created. The entire exercise is designed to take between fifteen and twenty minutes.

If you want, you can record the visualization word-for-word on an audiotape, which you can then play each time you wish to repeat the imagery. As you record the guidelines, speak in a slow, soothing voice, allowing approximately a minute of silence between each instruction. An alternative to an audiotape is to have someone you trust read the guidelines to you as you visualize. Rehearse the reading ahead of time, with you listening to make sure the tone and pace of the reader's voice are okay for the purpose.

Visualization for the Worrier Procrastinator

(1) Close your eyes and take a few deep breaths to relax your body—inhaling slowly through your nose, then exhaling slowly through your mouth. Let go of any tension or tightness in your body. Allow the thoughts and cares of the day to drift away, leaving your body light, your mind empty.

(2) In this relaxed state, picture yourself standing in the middle of a clearing in a densely wooded forest. Imagine yourself slowly turning in a circle on this spot, looking at the edge of the clearing as you turn. Notice that there are very few gaps between the trees and that you can't see very far into the forest.

(3)   Now stand still again and feel yourself become totally motionless, as if you were paralyzed. You want to go forward into the forest, but your body refuses to move. You feel more and more strain. Increase the muscular tension in your arms, your body, your legs. Let your anxiety level rise.

(4)   Now imagine you hear a gentle voice within the forest softly calling your name, over and over. As it continues to call, the tension slowly drains from your body, until it is all gone. You are still standing there, motionless, but now you are completely relaxed again.

(5)   Still relaxed and motionless, hear the voice continuing to call your name, gradually getting louder and clearer. You realize it is your own voice, at its strongest and most beautiful. Your voice stops, and then, several yards into the forest, you see someone coming toward you. As the figure slowly comes closer and closer to the clearing, you realize this figure is you, only looking much more positive and self-confident than you usually do.

(6)   See your "new self" walk into the clearing and come to a stop in front of you. Imagine yourself completely comfortable, standing face-to-face with your new self. Spend a few moments noticing the specific things about your new self that look different from the way you normally look: more positive, more self-confident. Perhaps, it's the expression in your eyes, the way you hold your body, or the clothing you're wearing.

(7)   Now imagine that you hear your new, more confident self say to you, "It's time for you to have more trust in yourself. Move out of your comfort zone and take a risk. You can handle more than you think. If you fall, I'll be there to catch you. If you get lost, I'll show you the way."

(8) Take these words into your heart. Savor the hope and encouragement that they give you. Feel confidence building in your body, like a sensation of warmth spreading from your heart. Then, imagine yourself slowly walking forward into the forest, all the while sensing the new you walking along side of you.

(9) Imagine that as you walk through the forest, the trees become farther and farther apart, and more and more sun shines through. Finally, you come to a big meadow —the end of the forest. You look up into the clear blue sky, filled with pride and contentment. Stay with this feeling as long as you wish, then slowly open your eyes.

2. *Avoid mentally "catastrophizing" tasks.*

Worrier procrastinators are inclined to dwell on the dreaded possibilities of a project or an event to the exclusion of everything else. This obsessive attention creates a false perspective: The projects or events themselves loom much larger than they actually are, and they take on a much more negative quality than they actually possess.

In thinking about a project or an event that you are facing, guard against your natural tendency to overestimate the time it will take, the energy you will have to expend, and the problems it will cause in your life. Wait until you can make an objective, realistic assessment of these matters before moaning and groaning. Meanwhile, why not be optimistic? This kind of attitude may even help you to see otherwise hidden ways of making the project easier—and less fearful.

3. *Recognize that making no decision is, in fact, making a decision.*

Putting things off because you can't decide what to do is an indirect decision not to do anything. And by not doing anything, you place yourself at the mercy of people who are more directly decisive. Is this what you want? Do you *really* want others to decide things for you? Do you *really* believe that they are more qualified to make decisions about your life than you are?

If your answer to any of these questions is "yes," then delve further into self-examination and ask yourself, "Why?" "Don't I believe that I'm capable?" "What am I avoiding by not making my own decisions?" Forcing yourself to answer questions like these will give you a clearer picture of your situation, so that you can be more forthright and constructive in your decision-making.

4. *When faced with something challenging, be sure to give as much consideration to what's exciting about it as you do to what's anxiety-provoking about it.*

There's a thin line between feeling nervous about something and feeling excited about it. Worrier procrastinators tend to lean toward the nervousness side of that line and away from the excitement side.

As you think about a project or an activity, reverse this pattern. When you find yourself concentrating on what's scary about something, shift your focus to what's exciting about it. The more you practice this shift, the more you'll discover that the two sensations have a lot in common. The major difference is in your interpretation of your bodily experience. The next time you have "butterflies in your stomach," think of it as a sign of excitement, not fear.

A related approach is to view challenging tasks as an opportunity to learn something new or have a new experience. Keep reminding yourself of why you initially thought it was a good idea to become involved in it, or, if that's not appropriate, why it's a good idea to perform it in a timely and efficient manner. Stay attuned to the full range of benefits that this project or activity can have for you, if you do it well—not the least of which will be a sense of accomplishment and an enhanced belief in yourself. The bottom line is to train yourself to look more at the opportunities than the difficulties of a situation.

5. *Learn to be your own best friend when you feel the need for encouragement or support.*

When faced with a challenging task or decision, worrier procrastinators too often run to someone else for help or comfort before they've sufficiently thought through the situation on their own. Thus, the message they give to themselves and to the other person only reinforces their low self-esteem: "I'm too scared or too incompetent; you do it for me."

Although it would be absurd and counterproductive to cut yourself off entirely from outside help, you need to resist the temptation to make it your first resort. Your first dialogue should be with yourself. Develop a self-nurturing part of your personality that tells you, "You can do this; just go over the facts of the matter, one by one. What are your options? What are your preferences? What personal talents and strengths can you apply here? What specific resources might you need?" This kind of inner dialogue will not only build your self-confidence but also assist you to talk more productively with others when—and if—you do wind up consulting with them.

6. *To help yourself become more decisive, follow a two-part decision-making process: first commit yourself to the goal, then determine the steps you'll take to achieve that goal.*

As a worrier procrastinator, you no doubt often have trouble deciding *whether* to do something because you can't decide *how* to do it. These should be two separate decisions, and it's best to make the former decision *before* you go on to consider the latter one. Otherwise, you'll keep yourself painfully—and fearfully—confused: overwhelmed with scary unknowns and, as a result, paralyzed with indecision.

Suppose, for example, you're putting off going for your master's degree because of the expense and time involved. Given this cart-before-the-horse logic, you have an excellent excuse to keep on procrastinating. The issues will never change: yes, getting a master's degree is expensive and time-consuming, so no, it's something you won't do. Before you realize it, you've created your own special *BUT* factor: "I'd like to get my master's degree, *BUT* it's too expensive and it takes too much time."

In fact, you're mixing up the *goal* with the *path to the goal*. The only way to straighten out the confusion—and, in doing so, break through your *BUT* factor—is to handle each decision-making step separately and in order. First and foremost, do you want to get your master's degree: yes or no? If you commit yourself once and for all to a "yes" answer, then a psychological hurdle has been cleared. You have a clear goal, and you can proceed to the various "how to" decisions that will help you reach that goal.

Once you apply yourself fearlessly to examining your "how to" options, you'll probably find that you have many more choices than you originally thought. With a master's degree as a goal, you can talk to financial advisers to work out a budget. There may be a grant you can apply for. Maybe you can borrow money from a bank or a relative, or get a part-time job, or work out a more flexible work schedule with your boss. Maybe you can find a master's program that doesn't take so much time. Whatever you decide, at least you've already decided to start!

CHANGING HOW YOU SPEAK

1. *Change your "I don't know"s to "One thing I do know is . . ."*

   The phrase "I don't know . . ." (as in "I don't know why I stay in this awful relationship") is often spoken by worrier procrastinators as a means of avoiding any deeper, more revealing assessment of a situation. In the first place, they don't want to articulate the specific, underlying fears or insecurities they may have; in the second place, they want to put off doing anything that might, somehow, turn out to be "wrong."

   Instead of simply tossing off this "I don't know" phrase, challenge yourself to say something bolder and more specific: "One thing I *do* know is . . ." For example, instead of "I don't know why I stay in this awful relationship," you might say, "One thing I *do* know is that I'm afraid to be alone" (or, "that I can't stand the way the other person runs my life for me," or "that I worry about hurting the other person's feelings"). Instead of, "I don't know how to fix the vacuum cleaner," you might say, "One thing I *do* know is that I'm worried about spending too much money this month" (or "that several of my friends are good at fixing things," or "that it bothers me that my carpet is getting so soiled").

2. *Change your "I can't" statements to compound sentences: "I can't . . . but I can . . ."*

   Another way of compelling yourself to become more assertive—and therefore less fearfully stuck in procrastination—is to replace simple "I can't" statements with more illuminating compound sentences such as "I can't . . . but

I can . . ." You will then be shifting the focus for yourself
and your listener away from what you *can't* do toward what
you *can* do. For example, instead of merely declaring, "I
can't quit my job now," say, "I can't quit my job now, but
I can start looking for other job possibilities" (or "take
courses so I can get a better job next year," or "ask my
boss for an assistant to help with the workload").

3. *Instead of panicking with a rhetorical "What if?" question,*
   go one step further and state the answer.

   Worrier procrastinators can easily get into the self-
defeating habit of using rhetorical "What if?" statements
to dramatize—and justify—their inactivity. For example,
suppose you continue to put off getting advance tickets for
a long-overdue vacation trip and explain your inactivity to
others by saying, "What if I'm too busy with work then?"
By leaving this statement hanging in the air, you're reinforcing your own blind anxiety about the future and indirectly asking your listener to "buy into" that anxiety.

   Instead, give yourself and your listener a break by answering your own question: "I'd have to arrange for someone else to do my work" or "I'd have to reschedule the trip
and accept a slight penalty fee." Even the worst-case
scenario—"I'd have to cancel my trip and lose a bundle
of money"—sounds much less ominous when it's spoken
out loud instead of left to ring, and echo, inside your
head.

4. *Instead of making an "I'm waiting . . ." statement, go one*
   step further and make a "meanwhile I'm doing . . ."
   statement.

   Whether or not they realize it, worrier procrastinators use
a lot of "waiting statements" to justify their inactivity and

mask their procrastination. "I'm waiting for the monthly sales report." "I'm waiting for better weather."

Don't let "waiting statements" escape from your lips without an additional, "meanwhile I'm doing" statement. "I'm waiting to find out what my friend does; meanwhile I'm developing several possible plans." "I'm waiting for the monthly sales report; meanwhile I'm doing the cost-benefit analysis for another project." "I'm waiting for better weather; meanwhile I'm cleaning and repairing my gear." The addition of a "meanwhile I'm doing" statement casts you as an achiever rather than a victim of circumstance.

5. *Reduce the number of qualifiers in your speech.*

Qualifiers are words and phrases like "maybe," "perhaps," "try to," "kind of," "practically," and "as much as I can." Be sensitive to the way you use qualifiers to make tentative statements—ones that dodge a firm commitment —and speak more affirmatively. Instead of, "I'll try to get it done," be more self-confident and say, "I'll get it done." Instead of "I'll read as much as I can today," be more definite and say, "I'll read fifty pages today" (or "half the book" or "the whole book").

CHANGING HOW YOU ACT

1. *Each day, do at least one thing that you've consciously been putting off.*

It doesn't need to be some big or complicated project that you hate to think about (although that would be great). If can be a little thing—a simple, quick task, like polishing a pair of shoes or answering a letter, or accomplishing a small part of a large project, like throwing away a few of your old, useless files (rather than reorganizing your entire filing system) or phoning friends who can bring chairs to a big party you're having (rather than making all the party arrangements at once). It can even be something you love doing but haven't let yourself do for some time, like walking through the woods or trying out a new recipe. The point is to be able to say to yourself, "I did it!" so that you can remind yourself how good it feels.

2. *Each week, do something that you're generally uncomfortable doing.*

As a worrier procrastinator, you need to expand your smaller-than-normal comfort zone, so you're more willing to engage in a broader range of activities and less likely to avoid things or procrastinate out of fear. Keep an ongoing list of all the activities you don't like doing, or are afraid to do, or feel you don't know how to do very well. Your list will no doubt include many different kinds of tasks: driving at night, learning new computer procedures, playing card games, talking with your father, doing household repairs, eating at a restaurant by yourself, going over the household budget. Then, every week, do one of these things *on your own initiative*—i.e., not because someone or something is forcing you to do it.

In many cases, you may find it helpful to act on one of your list items very impulsively, when your mood just happens to be right. Sometimes when you give the matter too much thought ahead of time, you talk yourself out of it. Assuming, for example, that you're afraid of flying, yet you may find yourself feeling especially courageous one afternoon. If so, just say to yourself, "What the hell!," pick up the phone, and book a flight in the near future to a place you've long wanted to visit.

3. *Read motivational books and develop a personal repertoire of motivational phrases.*

Equip yourself well to be your own best coach when you're tempted to procrastinate. Browse around in local bookstores and libraries for inspiring words to say at just the right moment of indecision, fearfulness, or discouragement.

One book I especially recommend for worrier procrastinators is Dr. Seuss's *Oh, the Places You'll Go.* It wonderfully describes and despicts the problems worrier procrastinators confront, as well as the spirit that's necessary to overcome those problems; and the rhyming language is easy—and delightful—to recall.

Children's books in general can be excellent motivators for adults, because so many of them have positive self-affirming messages. Such stories can help worried procrastinators to "reparent" themselves, offering them the healthy messages they wish they had received from their parents. These optimistic, comforting tales can help heal their wounded "inner child" who is still sabotaging their adult lives.

4. *Spend more time with optimistic people who inspire self-reliance, and less time with pessimistic people who foster neediness.*

Although it's usually a good idea to think through a challenging task or decision by yourself, there will be many times when you ultimately do need to get advice, support, reassurance, and brainstorming help from others. At these times, it's best if those to whom you turn are optimists, who believe in your abilities. Pessimists can increase your self-doubt and your tendency to procrastinate. For this reason, cultivate positive, self-encouraging relationships in your life, and avoid—or wean yourself away from—negative, self-crippling ones.

5. *Break down every large, intimidating project into an assortment of smaller, easier-to-do tasks.*

Worrier procrastinators tend to stun themselves into fearful inactivity by always looking at the big picture. Unfortunately, that can be overwhelming.

Why not divide that big picture into pieces, so it's easier on the mental eye? If you're faced with a task that seems overwhelming, follow this three-part strategy:

(1) Pick a date by which you want to have the whole task done.

(2) Make a list of all the small steps that are involved in that task.

(3) Plan to take only one, two, or a few steps at a time—it doesn't matter, as long as you've taken all the steps by the deadline you picked.

For example, if you have to write a résumé, you might subdivide that daunting task into a number of much less intimidating ones:

- making a list of your past jobs, in any format you want
- making a list of your work skills, in any format you want
- consulting books on writing résumés
- making a rough draft of a résumé, based on your reading
- showing your rough draft to other people who have written résumés
- revising your first draft, etc.

As you do each small task, you'll be more and more empowered—and motivated—to do the subsequent one. Always remember this truth: Doing creates the ability to do!

Chapter 5

The Defier
Procrastinator

". . . But why should I do it?"

The word "defier" conjures fierce, intimidating images: taut lips spitting out angry refusals; a clenched fist thrust into the air; an insolent face scowling above tightly crossed arms. Sometimes defier procrastinators actually present these images to the people in their lives; but much more often, they don't. As a matter of fact, they're more likely to display smiling lips saying just what you want to hear; open palms extended for a handshake of agreement; a kind face radiating cooperation. Far from flaunting their rebelliousness, most try to hide it under a guise of compliance. At times, they're convincing. At other times, they can't help sending a confusing mixed message of part agreement, part opposition.

We call these latter, more common defiers "passive-aggressive." They may say what others want to hear, but they don't do what they say. They may "shake on it," but they don't act on it. They may look ready and willing, but deep down, they're reluctant and resistant. Instead of active antagonism, their defiance takes a more slippery and subtle form—procrastination. They don't refuse to do things outright. They simply don't do them at all, or else they do them in an inefficient, uncaring manner.

The ongoing complaint of defier procrastinators, whether or not they express it verbally or even realize it consciously, is, "I could do it, *BUT* why should I do it?" The specific meaning of this complaint differs, depending on the situation. In some cases, it questions the importance of the task involved: ". . . *BUT* why *should* I do it?" In other cases, it implies that the task has been unfairly imposed upon them: ". . . *BUT* why should *I* do it?" Either way, they feel victimized and respond oppositionally.

Defier procrastinators tend to perceive any outside demand on their time and energy as a threat to their individuality. Depending on what type of personality they have, they may respond to that threat with outright indignation or with passive acceptance —as well as with procrastination.

Let's look first at an example of the *actively* aggressive defier procrastinator, who exhibits many of the openly rebellious images that we're inclined to associate with defiance. Mitch, a twenty-nine-year-old salesman, has an assertive, strong-willed personality that frequently helps him to nail a sale but also repeatedly causes him to lose jobs for not performing tasks in a timely or cooperative manner. When asked about these lapses, he either claims the jobs were "stupid to begin with" or blames someone else for causing problems. He rarely examines his own behavior to see how *he* may have made mistakes.

Outside of work, Mitch often behaves much like a toddler during the "terrible twos": full of spite, temper, and opposition aimed at anyone who challenges his power or authority. He's easily infuriated by bills and, therefore, highly likely to delay or resist paying them. He reacts to other people's requests in a similar manner, immediately arguing, "Don't go telling me what to do!" or "If you think it needs to be done so badly, then *you* do it."

Confronted with a task he dislikes, Mitch frequently refuses to do it, or else he goes about performing it in what he sarcastically calls "my own sweet time." He doesn't perceive that this type of procrastinating behavior is blameworthy. Instead, he sees it as a justifiable protest against being forced to give up his freedom or authority.

Mitch is just as stubborn and ornery in his personal relationships with others. He has never had a long-term relationship because he has ultimately antagonized every serious prospect. If not put off by his contentiousness and insensitivity, women have gotten fed up with the instability his chronic procrastination causes in his life.

Now let's turn from Mitch to the more common, if subtler, defier procrastinator: the passive-aggressive type. Amy is a fifty-two-year-old nurse who is overtly nice and helpful in every situation. She appears willing to do just about anything anyone asks her to do, and yet she has trouble actually doing just about everything. Time after time when a task needs to be done, she is slow to start or late to finish, and often she fails to act at all. Lacking introspection, she's baffled by why she so often finds herself in a jam, despite her good intentions.

Only people who are close to Amy comprehend what's really going on beneath her sweet, befuddled exterior. At first, she agrees to do something because it feels good to be agreeable. Later, it doesn't feel so good to face doing that thing, and the defier-procrastinator *BUT* factor takes over: ". . . *BUT* why should I do it?" She thus programs herself, consciously or unconsciously, not to do the task, or to do it halfheartedly because she's functioning against her will.

At home, Amy sometimes delays doing housework or puts off planning projects with her husband in a deliberate, if roundabout, effort to get back at him for his "superior airs" or his lack of attention. Usually, however, she remains unaware of how she employs passive-aggressive behavior to keep her loved ones in line. Meanwhile, much to their own and Amy's regret, her loved ones are obliged to keep their distance rather than get caught in Amy's web.

Once, Amy was an hour late in picking up her visiting daughter at the airport. Her tossed-off explanation was "A friend of mine was freaking out, and I couldn't just leave her." Not wanting to rekindle past conflicts, her daughter only chided Amy jokingly. Nevertheless, Amy was offended. "I can't understand why she was so upset," she said to her husband that night. "I was all tied up helping my friend. So she was waiting for me— so what? I've always told her you have to be kind to those who need you."

In this incident, as in many others, Amy refused to face her responsibility for her daughter's feelings, her lack of self-discipline, and her confused priorities. All too often she is like the fabled shoemaker whose children went without shoes: She is going to do what she is going to do, whether or not it is really the wisest thing to do, and whether or not her loved ones, or herself, wind up suffering for it. She doesn't actively intend to be mean by procrastinating, but she is being defiant in a passive-aggressive manner.

We've just taken a brief look at the two categories of defier procrastination—active and passive-aggressive. Now let's consider what characteristics *all* defier procrastinators have in common:

1. *Defier procrastinators see life in terms of what others expect or require them to do, not in terms of what they themselves want or need to do.*

   Defier procrastinators are ever on the alert to avoid, resist, or fight against doing anything that someone else seems to be compelling them to do. This self-protective attitude keeps them focused on other people instead of themselves. As a result, they have a very poor sense of what, specifically, would make them happy or improve the quality of their day-to-day life. They might claim, "I just want to be left in peace," but ironically, they are responsible for their own lack of peace because of their defensive preoccupation with others.

What defier procrastinators fail to realize is that many of the tasks that appear to be "unfairly" imposed upon them from outside are in fact things they authentically need to do to lead a happy, productive life. Often, these dreaded tasks may be things they'd enjoy doing, if they weren't so predisposed to reject them.

Mitch, for example, is his own worst enemy when it comes to achieving satisfaction in a job or a relationship. By withholding full cooperation with one boss after another, and one lover after another, he's only hurting himself. He's like a small child battling his parents' helpful suggestions for self-management because he doesn't want to grow up. He doesn't give enough consideration to the fact that he might actually like growing up.

Amy subconsciously refuses to set up and follow priorities in her daily schedule because she doesn't want to feel that she has to put any boundaries on her moment-by-moment freedom to do what she wants to do. She doesn't see that she's thereby making herself a slave to her impulses, nor does she realize that she's thereby jeopardizing the relationships that are the nearest and dearest to her heart.

2. *In order to appear nice or cooperative, defier procrastinators often avoid expressing negative feelings directly and, instead, convey them indirectly by procrastinating.*

This pattern is most apparent and consistent in the case of a passive-aggressive defier, like Amy. We see it, for example, in the way she responds to conflicts she has with her husband. She can't bring herself to confront him openly and honestly about how she feels, because it would mean sacrificing her accommodating, "good guy" self-image. She is also resistant to any negotiation that might force her to revise her self-justifying "bad guy" image of him. So what does she do? She retaliates *passively* by being slow to fulfill her household responsibilities or to cooperate with her husband in making joint plans.

This self-conflicting pattern of projecting a positive front while harboring negative feelings also occurs in the lives of predominantly active defier procrastinators, like Mitch. Face-fo-face with his clients, Mitch strives to appear much more agreeable, compliant, and useful than he truly is—or even needs to be—in order to secure their business. Later, to "get even" for having had to put on this act, he is slow to provide service, although he usually doesn't recognize that this is what's happening. If he'd learn to be more honest with his clients right from the start, and more honest with himself about his intentions and obligations, he'd become a more "real" and effective long-term salesperson.

3. *Defier procrastinators resent authority and use procrastination as a means of challenging it.*

Defier procrastinators get upset whenever they think that another individual—or society as a whole—is trying to tell them what to do. They take it as a threat to their self-importance. In fact, they wouldn't feel so threatened by this outside challenge if they didn't have so much trouble telling *themselves* what to do; but they don't see this. They see only that they're being pressured, that the pressure is undeserved, and that their self-esteem somehow demands that they fight back.

Sometimes defier procrastinators perceive their resistance to authority as an exciting battle against boring conformity. Thus, they complain that social obligations or rituals are actually contemptible efforts to make them just like everybody else, when they want to be special. Mitch scoffs at following company rules—or even paying his bills—for just this reason.

Other times, defier procrastinators are more subtle in flouting conventional expectations. For example, Amy— only half aware of what she was doing—used a friend's sudden need as an excuse for not showing up at the airport in time to pick up her daughter: something that society might expect a parent should do, and something that her daughter had assumed she would do. Amy's passive-aggressive act of rebellion against such expectations was also a means of making herself special in a situation that would otherwise have made her daughter special.

4. *Defier procrastinators are pessimistic by nature, which undercuts their motivation to do things in a timely, effective manner.*

Always feeling put upon, defier procrastinators view life in general as "unfair." This attitude gives them a right to rebel, and a rationale for procrastination. Hence, Mitch somehow accepts the fact that he'll always have trouble holding a job. To him, it's the inevitable fate of someone who is a "true individual" rather than a "phony conformer." Therefore, he won't even think about changing his defier-procrastinator behavior—which is, in fact, the actual cause of the trouble.

In a similar fashion, Amy thinks of herself as the perpetually misunderstood "good guy" at the mercy of self-righteous "bad guys." She doesn't appreciate that life would probably be a whole lot better, and certainly less combative, if she would only start changing the way she thinks. She could then go on to change the way she acts, which would really make a difference.

5. *Defier procrastinators resist performing the kind of thoughtful self-assessment that might help them see their problems more clearly.*

Although defier procrastinators are quick to read faults, impositions, and offenses into people's motives and behaviors, they are blind to their dependence upon others. Because of their chronic procrastination, they force the people in their lives—especially those who are closest to them—to take on the thankless role of their caretakers and to cope with their unceasing, unacknowledged irresponsibility.

Defier procrastinators don't want to acknowledge their dependency on others, because it would be too humiliating for them. Regrettably, they often don't need to own up to it, precisely because the other people in their lives are silently, if grudgingly, making up for their deficiencies. Whenever another person in their lives *does* speak up, pointing out their self-destructive patterns, defier procrastinators feel misunderstood and defend themselves by blocking out any constructive criticism that's offered. It's a response that's become automatic to them, and it occurs even when it's not in their own best interest.

Mitch, the active defier, adamantly resists looking inside himself for the reasons he's unable to keep a job or develop a lasting personal relationship. Instead, he lashes out at others, assigning all the fault to them. Amy, the passive-aggressive defier, keeps herself mystified as to why she's so often "misunderstood." She doesn't question her own role in a misunderstanding, nor does she subject her behavior to frank and open discussions with others. She would rather be passively aggressive than openly confrontational.

All these characteristics combine and reinforce each other in the life of a "typical" passive-aggressive procrastinator, who also displays active defiance in some situations. Bill, a former client of mine who was a forty-two-year-old small-business owner, fits this profile.

BILL: THE DEFIER PROCRASTINATOR

Bill exhibited defier tendencies from the moment he entered my office. "Frankly, I'm here because I promised my wife I'd come," he announced rather testily, "but I'm not sure what to say or what you can do for me." It turned out that Bill was currently going through two crises of his own making: The Internal Revenue Service was charging him with tax evasion because he hadn't filed an income tax return for three years, and he was being forced to pay the total cost of a recent surgical operation because he'd let his health insurance lapse.

Both dilemmas were a direct result of Bill's ongoing tendency to procrastinate, but he didn't acknowledge this fact. Despite admitting that he was "technically at fault" for the two crises, he refused to take the blame entirely, insisting that they were cases of "big institutions squeezing the little guy."

Bill's wife, Suzanne, however, saw things differently. She had reached her limit of tolerance for his procrastination as well as for his misplaced accusations. The double whammy of the IRS suit and the lapsed insurance was threatening not only their financial security but also their marriage. Her respect for her husband, and her trust in him, was swiftly eroding, to the point where even he couldn't ignore or deny the need for change. Thus, he finally came to me; and I, too, sometimes found myself on the receiving end of his diatribes against other people's "unreasonable" demands.

Occasionally during our first few sessions together, Bill got so carried away by self-righteous anger that he failed to realize how irrational he was being. "I don't see why I have to be responsible to other people for what I do. It's my right to live my life the way I want to. If someone's unhappy about what I do, that's their problem, not mine."

As time went by, Bill began to speak of his procrastination problems more rationally. Though still defiant, he exhibited a passive-aggressive manner that indicated a certain amount of growing objectivity. For example, he once described to me a typical argument between himself and his wife in a way that demonstrated he was at least somewhat capable of appreciating her point of view:

> Suzanne will get ticked off about some small thing I've forgotten or haven't got around to yet, and then she'll say to me, "You're always putting things off! You never do what you say you'll do."
>
> And then I'll laugh—I don't know why, I guess to lighten her up a little—and I'll say, "Okay, once in a while I don't do something. What's the big deal?"
>
> Well, that only makes her angrier, and she'll say, "Nothing's *ever* a big deal with you. Whenever I ask you to do something, you say you're too busy, but you're busy with nothing. You'll tell me it's not the right time, but the right time never comes. I always wind up having to do it myself!"

In recounting the rest of this particular argument, Bill paused to confess that sometimes he did deliberately "bait" his wife by not doing what she wanted him to do, or by making her wait for him to do something. "I know it's not very nice," he pointed out, "but it *does* give me a sense of power. It shows me that I'm important to her, and a lot of times that's the only way I can tell."

This last remark only prompted yet another passive-defiant complaint. "If I started doing *everything* she expected me to do," Bill insisted, with irritation in his voice, "she'd expect me to do even more." Eventually, he worked himself up into a blanket criticism of *her* alleged need to get angry with him:

> I can't believe how trivial some of the things are that she gets mad at me about. She keeps harping that I haven't done this, or I haven't done that, and I'm determined not to cooperate with her anger. All I can say is, "Don't tell me you're going to get angry about *that* again!" I want her to see how ridiculous it is to be bothered by something so insignificant, time after time after time.

What Bill did not see—until later in his therapy—was the grave seriousness of *his* defier-procrastinator problem. Nor did he understand the many ways that it legitimately frustrated and even enraged the people around him, who would inevitably come to feel ignored, belittled, and manipulated by him.

There was, however, a ray of hope for Bill: He was utterly exhausted by the problem. "This me-against-the-world fight used to bring me a lot of satisfaction," he confided to me after the first month of therapy, "but lately it hasn't had that effect at all. I still do it, but it causes me tremendous stress. My stomach's in knots, I don't sleep well, and I look like hell."

Procrastination on the Job

Bill ran a small office-supplies business with three full-time and five part-time employees. The work itself was not that rewarding, but being his own boss was. "It got to the point where I just couldn't work for someone else," he said. "My last employer was the worst ever. Anything he told me to do, I automatically wouldn't want to do. And anything he told me *not* to do, I'd automatically want to do. I started my own business so that I could do whatever I wanted to do, when I wanted to do it."

Bill seemed obsessed with what he *wanted* to do, at the expense of what he *needed* to do. To lead a happy, productive life, a person's two objectives—doing what one wants and doing what needs to be done—should be fairly close to each other, but for Bill, they were almost diametrically opposed. He resented having to *need* to do anything; and as a result, he placed such an inflated value on getting what he *wanted* that he was chronically dissatisfied and frustrated.

As it turned out, becoming a boss was not as much fun or as liberating as Bill had imagined. Rather than blaming himself for having such a hopelessly vague, unrealistic attitude about "fun," "freedom," or "bosshood," he found every reason he could to blame the economy, the office-supplies industry, his employees, and his customers. One day he confessed to me, "I sometimes get so mad at other people that I can't calm down enough to do the day-by-day things that I know I should do. It means I have to do everything the hard way, at the last minute, which doesn't do my attitude any good!"

It also didn't do Bill's employees any good. He paid them well, but his managerial style constantly aggravated them. Although he considered himself above the rules, regulations, and schedules he set for his business, he expected his employees to follow them scrupulously, regardless of his bad example, and pounced on them when they didn't. He thought he was acting boldly and powerfully, as a strong executive should. Instead, he was *reacting* like an automaton, giving in to his built-in, defier-procrastinator *BUT* factor: ". . . *BUT* why should *I* have to supervise them? They should know what to do."

As far as Bill was concerned, steady, earnest, nuts-and-bolts work was for other people, not him. Determined to be special, he was oblivious to the fact that being special did not always lead to being happy or successful.

Procrastination at Home

As I mentioned earlier, Bill's personal life was in chaos by the time he came to me for therapy, mainly because of his procrastinating habits. His wife, unable to cajole, argue, or browbeat him into changing his ways, was on the verge of leaving him, and he faced the IRS suit and the huge medical bill.

Nevertheless, Bill's only response to these matters and to other difficulties in his personal life was to cling all the more tenaciously to the defiant attitudes that had brought him so much trouble in the first place. Whether he was talking to me about his marriage, his finances, his friendships, or his household routines, he'd repeat the same phrase over and over again: "I'll be damned if I'm going to let people push me around!"

Bill's personal rebellion against the Internal Revenue Service was especially instructive about the way he'd serve as his own worst enemy. For most of his working life, he had been entitled to tax *refunds*, but even so, he had refused to file a return by the April 15 deadline. "I hate the idea that I have to do *anything* by a specific, arbitrary date," he said to me, as if that were a fully satisfactory explanation. "I want to do it when it makes sense to *me* to do it!"

This type of intransigent mind-set is especially difficult to change. Indeed, its very purpose is to deny that change is necessary, desirable, or valuable. Thus, in Bill's case, it prevailed even when his tax situation changed so that he owed the IRS money and faced legal and financial penalties if he didn't pay that money in a timely manner.

In his relationship with Suzanne, Bill was committed to a similarly defiant path, although he was a bit less like a lion and more like a lamb when talking about it. "It isn't just her that's the problem," he blurted out one day. "I find it constitutionally hard, seemingly harder than most people do, to keep track of schedules and deadlines that others have made for me. So I'm usually late doing anything she wants done, or showing up for anything she wants to do. And then I feel guilty, and then I get mad!"

Bill had always had this defiance-related problem in his intimate relationships. As a result, he had procrastinated marrying for years while he privately agonized over the loneliness and lack of love in his life. He waited until he was thirty-six to marry Suzanne, whom he had dated since he was thirty-one. "I felt the way many men do," he explained, "that women have no power over you until you marry them. And you know what? I *still* feel that way."

However irrational and limiting this point of view was, it continued to seem accurate to Bill because he himself continued to legitimize it. Whenever he disappointed Suzanne by being late or by not doing what she'd expected him to do (or even what he'd willingly volunteered to do), he would automatically cast her in the role of his adversary. It was *she* who was going to be upset and, therefore, who was going to dole out punishment. *He* would thus become the victim unless he fought back. Often, the only power that he felt he possessed to combat her power of "rightness" was a power of "wrongness"—an obstinate refusal to behave in an effective, responsible way.

How It All Started

Bill grew up admiring defiance and procrastination as easy methods for getting his own way. He dreaded turning into someone like his father, a printer who worked slavishly and unimaginatively and who, in Bill's eyes, was always being pushed around by his customers. He also feared being controlled by a woman the way his mother controlled both him and his father—by wheedling, scolding, and withholding her affection.

Throughout his childhood and early adolescence, Bill often felt terribly overburdened by his father's insistence that he work hard and his mother's demands that he do as she said. Sometimes, he developed enough courage to defy his parents openly, but often he could not. After all, his parents were stronger than he was, and like any child, he craved their approval. So he would appear to be compliant with their wishes, hoping to placate them at least for the time being, and then he would rebel covertly by procrastinating.

Over the years, Bill taught himself a wide variety of slippery, passive-aggressive responses to his parents' inquiries:

- "I'll get to it in a minute, Mom" (never giving it a second thought)
- "But Dad, my room *is* clean!" (staring down any contrary opinion with a fierce look of incredulity)
- "I'm doing it right now, Mom!" (arranging the books for his homework assignment and then walking away a moment later)
- "Don't worry about the mess in the toolshed, Dad!" (taking care not to state any specific clean-up time)
- "I'll think about it, Mom" (avoiding any "yes" commitment)
- "I have to do a few other things first, Dad" (giving himself the freedom never to get around to the requested task)

The hierarchical, task-driven nature of school only helped Bill to hone his passive-aggressive behavioral skills. In performing assignments and dealing with the teachers' deadlines, he learned to dance a daring pattern of defiance (procrastinating) and accommodation (meeting a deadline at the last minute, or getting an extension, or missing it altogether without serious consequence).

Every now and then, Bill would suffer a major setback at

school—a course failed, a scholastic opportunity lost, a chance for self-fulfillment missed—usually because at some point he became *actively* defiant toward a teacher he disliked and was called to account for that. But the system as a whole curiously enabled him to survive with all his *passive* aggressiveness intact.

The phenomenon continued to hold true for Bill in the business world. For years, he managed to sustain himself through aggressiveness or manipulation rather than through a more positive, efficient use of his time and energy. Now time had run out on him, in terms of both his productive life as a businessman and his personal life as a human being.

Changing the Pattern

During the first few months of therapy, it became apparent to me and even to Bill that many of his defiance-related procrastination problems developed from a lack of self-awareness. He didn't see the absurdity in many of his thoughts and statements about other people trying to "push him around." He also wasn't able to differentiate between those rare times when someone was pushing him around and those frequent times when he created a defiant scenario all on his own.

To become more conscious of the problems he was creating for himself, Bill began keeping a written record of the times when he found himself thinking, speaking, or acting in an "agitated" or "trouble-causing" manner. Gradually, he taught himself to recognize the specific thoughts or verbal expressions that signaled danger, like, "How dare he!" or "Who does he think he is?" or "I don't deserve this kind of treatment!" or "I'll show them!"

Bill also identified specific gestures and deeds that were closely associated with his self-destructive pattern of defiant procrastination, like stabbing with his index finger to emphasize statements of resistance, or refusing to look at papers and letters that might require some response on his part. Eventually, he was able to tell when he was on the verge of possibly making trouble for himself and, therefore, to prevent that trouble from happening.

At the same time that Bill was learning to appreciate his tendency toward self-destructiveness, he also needed to learn better ways of nurturing his self-esteem, so that he wouldn't seek so hard to prove himself right by proving others wrong. In short, he needed to counterbalance his campaign of healthy self-criticism with some specific effort toward healthy self-gratification.

One of Bill's biggest successes in this endeavor came at work. In addition to his supervisory duties as a boss (which, so far, he had tended to execute in an abusive manner), he took on the personal, solitary task of revising the company's billing procedures to make them more efficient. Through designing and developing a better billing system, he gained not only a stronger, more lasting sense of self-worth but also (a surprise bonus!) a more tolerant perspective on billing systems in general. This reframed point of view helped him become less defiant and more time-sensitive about paying his own debts.

Bill's story is unique to him in many respects, but it contains elements that are common to all defier procrastinators, most notably a destructive preoccupation with other people at the expense of a constructive self-awareness. Now it's time for you to take a closer look at your own unique story of defier procrastination, so that you, too, can transform your life for the better.

HOW TO STOP BEING A DEFIER PROCRASTINATOR

The most important single step toward overcoming defier procrastination lies in shifting your concern away from what other people might be doing to you and toward what you might be doing to yourself. Here's a self-assessment exercise to help you start making this shift:

1. Recall at least two different occasions when you were faced with a project or activity that you *wanted or needed to do BUT never did* out of defiance. For each occasion, ask yourself these questions:
   • Whom was I defying, and why?
   • What were the consequences to myself of not doing it? What were the consequences to others?

2. Recall at least two different occasions when you *finished something BUT wasted time or got it done late* because you were caught up in defiance. For each occasion, ask yourself:
   • Whom, specifically, was I defying, and why?
   • What were the consequences of my wasting time or being late? How did it make me feel? What effect did it have on my relationships?

The solution to your personal defiance-related procrastination problems lies not only in cultivating greater self-awareness, on an ongoing basis, but also in translating what you learn into more constructive, self-nurturing thoughts, words, and deeds. Therefore, it's important to utilize all three aspects of the self-improvement program outlined below: thinking, speaking, and acting.

CHANGING HOW YOU THINK

1. *Practice creative visualization.*
    Defier procrastinators need to cultivate a richer, more satisfying inner life to keep them from focusing so

intently—and self-destructively—on other people. One of the best ways to do this is to practice visualization on a regular basis.

At first, it may be difficult for you to "see" clear images with your mind's eye as you follow the guidelines of a visualization. If this is the case, try the best you can to experience thoughts, shapes, colors, and feelings that relate to the imagery. With repeated practice, you'll soon be able to visualize more easily.

Creative visualization is a skill that's very much worth the effort of acquiring. By training your imagination to develop more vivid mental pictures of who you are and what you want, you'll gain more self-confidence and a greater sense of aliveness. As a result, you'll be much better equipped to deal with life in a constructive manner rather than a defiant one.

The visualization exercise that appears below is one that I created specifically to help defier procrastinators become more even-tempered and productive. First, read it all the way through several times, until you feel you know it fairly well. Bear in mind that you do not need to recall it word for word, or detail for detail, as it is written here. It's sufficient simply to be able to recall the overall structure.

When you feel you've got the gist of the visualization, go ahead and try it out. Assume a comfortable position somewhere that is quiet, dimly lit, and free from distraction. Some people prefer lying down with their legs straight and slightly apart, and their arms extended loosely at their sides; others prefer to relax in a comfortable chair or on a couch. Then, silently speak the guidelines to yourself, as you remember them. Go all the way through the visualization scenario at a slow, relaxed pace. Make sure to allow at least a minute of quiet visualization time between instructions. The entire exercise is designed to take between fifteen and twenty minutes.

If you wish, you can record the guidelines as printed (except for the words between parentheses in number 3) on an audiotape. Then you can replay this audiotape later, whenever you choose to practice the visualization. As you record the guidelines, speak in a slow, soothing voice, allowing approximately a minute of silence between instructions. An alternative to an audiotape is to have someone read the guidelines to you, in the same relaxing manner, as you actually perform the visualization.

Visualization for the Defier Procrastinator

(1)   Close your eyes and take a few deep breaths to relax your body—inhaling slowly through your nose, then exhaling slowly through your mouth. Let go of any tension or tightness in your body. Allow the thoughts and cares of the day to drift away, leaving your body light, your mind empty.

(2)   Start going back through time, pausing at different stages of your life to recall a few images of what you were like. Now, imagine yourself when you were twenty-one. Remember what you looked like, what you often felt like, what you liked to do. Then go back to when you were sixteen. Then return to when you were twelve. Finally, imagine yourself as a young child around five years old, just before you started first grade.

(3)   Remaining at this last age, imagine yourself doing something that you liked to do then to feel happy and smart (e.g., coloring a picture, solving a puzzle, building a house with blocks). As you continue this activity, notice

how good it makes you feel about yourself, how energized you are.

(4) Gradually bring this activity to a conclusion, and allow yourself a few moments of pleasure and pride about having done it.

(5) Now slowly return to your present age. Imagine yourself choosing, of your own free will, to do something that brings you similarly positive feelings. Make it a fairly simple activity that you can complete in a relatively short amount of time. You start doing this activity, feeling good about it.

(6) You continue performing this activity at a relaxed but steady pace, becoming increasingly involved as you go along. Imagine yourself gaining more and more self-satisfaction from it, even though some parts of it may be routine or difficult.

(7) Now imagine yourself finishing this activity. After you've finished, pause a few moments and take pride in what you've accomplished. Feel good that you set aside the time to do this task and that you directed your energy toward it in such a rewarding way—without resentment or resistance. Savor the new energy and enthusiasm for life that you're now experiencing, thanks to what you've done.

(8) Now picture a specific task in your present life that you do *not* want to do but that you realize needs to be done—a task that is also relatively short. Imagine choosing to do this task of your own free will, and then go about performing it in the same relaxed but steady way in which you undertook the previous activity.

(9) Now see yourself finishing this activity and feeling good about what you've done. Take pride in the fact that you

chose to do this activity without feeling hassled or pressured by someone else. Feel powerful and pleased that you completed it without experiencing resentment or resistance.

(10) Now hear a voice within you saying, "You can choose to do a job well, even if someone else gave you that job, because doing it well can make you feel good about yourself." Pause a moment to realize the truth of these words, and when you're ready, slowly open your eyes.

2. *Learn to view what someone else wants or expects as a request, not a demand.*

Defier procrastinators are inclined to look upon every message from the outside world as an attack on their right to remain completely independent. In fact, we are all dependent upon outside people (e.g., family, coworkers, policemen) for our very survival, and therefore it's usually in our own best interests to be as cooperative with these people as we can reasonably be. Naturally, we want to cooperate *on our own terms* as much as we can, but we won't really be able to work out these terms with other people if we're constantly defying them.

As a defier procrastinator, you probably find it difficult to accept directions from others and view them as intrusions on your freedom. "Okay," you instantly say to yourself, "Someone's making a demand upon me, and I resent it!" For your own peace of mind (as well as everyone else's), you need to train yourself not to be so defensive right from the start. Instead of unwittingly reacting with rebellion whenever someone asks you to do something, deliberately enlarge your options by saying to yourself, "Okay, this is a *request* from someone else. How shall I respond?"

3. *Generate multiple options for response to each situation you encounter.*

Defier procrastinators are in the habit of entertaining only three crude response options for every situation:

(1) *comply as indicated*, in which case they are viewed as nice and cooperative but lose their own sense of freedom and individuality;

(2) *defy in an active manner*, in which case they are viewed unfavorably but maintain their own sense of freedom and individuality; or

(3) *defy in a passive-aggressive manner*, in which case they may initially be viewed favorably and, at the same time, maintain some sense of their own freedom and individuality, but most assuredly, they will eventually be viewed as manipulative and selfish.

To break this habit in your life, you need to approach each new situation as a creative challenge, calling for you to generate a full range of possible responses. You can then exercise your individuality by choosing the one particular response that you judge to be the most appropriate. In the long run, this type of expanded decision-making is bound to be more self-satisfying and productive than blindly setting into motion one of the three "automatic pilot" options already mentioned.

For example, let's suppose your employer has assigned you an additional report to prepare every month. Without giving it much constructive thought, you're likely to respond in one of the three basic defier-procrastinator ways: (1) go ahead and do it as asked, hating every minute of it; (2) blow up at your boss for unfairly increasing your workload; or (3) say a polite "yes" to your boss, then stash the report request at the very bottom of your work pile. Whichever of these three things you do, you'll wind up feeling bad about yourself, your work, and your employer.

Now consider how much better it would be if you could apply some constructive thought to the situation *before* going on automatic pilot. Here are just some of the more positive response options you might generate:

- Investigate with your boss the possibility of composing a shorter, less complicated report than originally requested.
- Discuss with your boss the possibility of turning in the report bimonthly instead of monthly.
- Propose to your boss the possibility of having more lead time before the first report is due, and of doing the report for a limited, three-month trial period instead of for an indefinite period of time.
- Figure out parts of the report that you might be able to delegate effectively to others, whom you supervise (including possible part-time or temporary help authorized by your boss).
- Negotiate with your boss to be relieved of some of your regular work responsibilities so that you have more time for the report.
- Figure out several different, more comfortable ways of doing the report than originally requested and submit them to your boss for consideration.

Above all, you need to be *specific and solution-oriented* rather than *global and resistance-oriented* in your response to an outside directive. This means curbing your immediate predisposition to overreact. By appraising each situation coolly and logically before determining how you'll respond, you increase your control over what you eventually do, and feel less forced to do something according to someone else's rules.

4. *Recognize when you're starting to burn with indignation and, instead, start thinking in a calmer, more practical manner about the best course of action.*

Pay attention to how you think and feel when you're confronted by an outside request, learning to appreciate the signals that you may be overreacting. Does your mind immediately start racing with reasons *not* to do what's being asked? Do you clench your fists? Do you start talking angrily to yourself? Do you fantasize impossible revenge scenarios? Once you know your personal danger signals, you can stop drifting toward defier procrastination and take a better, more masterful direction.

5. *Pick your battles carefully, weighing what's really worth fighting for according to a scale of priorities.*

Defiance consumes energy. Even if your "act" of defiance is not to do anything at all, your mind remains fixated on images of some outside person or system as the oppressor and you as the victim. This kind of "victim mentality" limits your sense of personal autonomy, which automatically provokes even more defiance.

If, instead of allowing yourself to feel victimized, you cultivate a stronger, more capable sense of self, you no longer experience such a compulsion to defy. You can then *choose* to defy when it's truly appropriate, rather than every time you encounter an outside demand.

Guard against expending too much of your energy on defiance, saving it for the truly worthwhile fights. There will be situations in which a defiant response is both pragmatic and self-preserving, such as refusing to pay for a job that's

only partially done, or fighting back against a false accu-
sation that could harm your reputation. However, there are
many situations where a defiant response is likely to hurt
you much more than its intended target, such as refusing
to pay legitimate bills that you owe, or procrastinating on
agreed-upon work projects.

6. *Develop an internal "nurturing parent" who tells you what's
best to do and gives you a better sense of self.*

In your dialogues with yourself, imagine that you have a
gentle, nurturing parent inside you. This ideal parent is not
someone who is harsh, critical, or quick to berate you for
what you haven't done, but someone who speaks with wis-
dom and maturity, motivating you to do the things that you
need to do.

Cultivate this nurturing parent by being gentle and ra-
tional, rather than angry and polemical, in your self-
dialogue. When you're faced with a task that you resist
doing, ask this part of you specific questions regarding how,
where, what, why, when, and even whether to do it, instead
of complaining about the task as a whole in an exaggerated,
histrionic fashion.

Think of this nurturing parent as a resource that can
help make things better, as long as you're open and honest
in using it. Whenever you're stuck in a defiant, self-
destructive rut not wanting to do something, that nurturing
mom or dad can remind you of some essential truths you
might otherwise be too wrapped up in your defiance to appreciate, namely:

• Not everything needs to feel good in order for you to
do it.
• There are many things you need to do that won't feel
good.

- Something that feels good in the short term (like putting off a task you don't like) may turn out to be bad for you in the long term.
- Something that feels bad in the short term (like applying yourself to a task you don't like) may turn out to be good for you in the long term.

CHANGING HOW YOU SPEAK

1. *Mean what you say.*

When it comes to talking about what you'll do and when you'll do it, don't just say what other people might want to hear in order to get them off your back. Those words might well return to haunt you! Instead, give importance to what you say by being careful to state only what you truly intend to do and by silently pledging your commitment to that intention once it's been spoken.

If you later feel the need to modify what you've said, then take responsibility for the modification in a direct statement to the person or people involved. For example, you might say, "I know I told you I'd take care of it this week, but I didn't realize at the time how much I was already obligated to do." If possible, offer another, more certain deadline at the same time—and mean what you say!

2. *Avoid words of blame or attack.*

One of the major lessons that a defier procrastinator needs to learn is not to be so quick to use confrontational language to deflect unwanted requests or criticism: "You're always nagging at me to do things!" "You're never satisfied!" "You're only thinking of yourself!" It may make you feel temporarily powerful to hurl accusations at the other person, but it only escalates the conflict and inflames that person's anger against you even further.

Try making statements that begin with "I" instead of "you" when you express your negative feelings: "I feel as if I'm being hounded to do things." "I get upset when you find fault with something that I think I've done well." "I feel misunderstood and think that you don't appreciate my point of view." When you talk about *your* feelings, and begin your statements with "I," it will help to make the other person less defensive and more willing to see things from your perspective.

3. *If you haven't done something, own up to it.*

You're only asking for trouble if you allow the other person to assume that you're doing what you agreed to do when, in fact, you're not. Even if the other person never actually calls you to account for your procrastination, you'll be adding to your own store of personal guilt and undermining your self-esteem.

In any situation where you haven't performed as expected, let the other person know in an honest and timely manner, without making up an excuse or launching a counterattack. If an apology is in order, make it a direct one (e.g., "I'm sorry I haven't finished it yet") rather than an indirect one in which you dodge any personal responsibility (e.g., "I'm sorry that you're upset about this").

Defier procrastinators often dread apologizing because they equate an apology with an admission of having been stupid, lazy, or bad. Indeed, your fear of possibly having to apologize may frequently account for your extreme defensiveness. You need to realize that an apology is simply a courtesy, a reaffirmation of personal responsibility, and (in some cases) a prelude toward renegotiating terms.

When delivering an apology, take care not to fly to the other extreme from defiance by collapsing into self-laceration: "I feel so horrible! I never do anything right!" Instead, briefly express your regret, and (if appropriate) follow it up with a pledge toward some sort of specific, positive action in the future: "I'm sorry I didn't get this done by Monday. I'll have it for you by Thursday." And then do it!

Finally, avoid getting into too many situations where an apology is—or might be—necessary. Repetitive apologizing without significant reform is part of the passive-aggressive syndrome.

4. *Minimize expressions of indignation or self-righteousness.*

Eliminate the following defiant phrases (and others like them) from your speaking vocabulary: "Don't tell me"; "What gives you the right"; "How dare you"; "I'm not the one, you are"; "You can't expect me to." Instead, speak in a manner that's more temperate and open to cooperation, staying focused on facts, not personalities, and solutions, not accusations.

5. *Be aware of your tone of voice, and try not to sound confrontational.*

Listen to yourself when you speak. Regardless of what your *words* say, does your *voice* sound hostile, challenging, exasperated, hesitant, doubtful, condescending, mean-spirited, sarcastic? Is it somehow at odds with your words, conveying a more negative, defiant message than they do?

The same words said in a snide tone can convey an entirely different meaning than if they were spoken in a sincere tone. To avoid any misunderstandings—and, therefore, possible confrontations—your voice should match your words and should *not* be used as a secret weapon. Accepting responsibility for how you sound is the first step toward making your vocal tone, in general, more positive and constructive.

CHANGING HOW YOU ACT

1. *Always strive to act rather than react.*

Take pains to "decide and do" rather than "complain and defy." The former approach puts you in charge, while the latter leaves the other person in control.

To remember this guideline more vividly, associate it with a "powerful adult" vs. "impotent child" analogy. In any task-related situation, an *adult* is someone who is powerful enough to work out an action plan that gives him or her the freedom to function as a mature, independent agent. A *child,* by contrast, is someone who is relatively powerless and therefore whose only options are to obey or rebel (either directly or indirectly). These images can help inspire you to behave more like a powerful adult and less like an impotent child.

If you can't help but feel irritable or resistant about doing something, don't simply hide that feeling so that it can continue to bother you. Instead, say something constructive and cooperative that will help others understand what's concerning you. Is it something that's not fair? Do you feel left out of the decision-making process? Is the timing likely to cause problems with your schedule? Work on improving what I call your "response ability"—your ability to respond by expressing yourself to others in an open and constructive manner so that you can work jointly at finding solutions to problems.

2. *Do what you know needs to be done.*

Mentally engrave this motto into the forefront of your consciousness! Keep track of what needs to be done, even if it means literally writing it down and posting it someplace you can't overlook, and then follow through as stated. It's not so much a matter of appeasing someone else as holding yourself accountable to yourself.

If you commit to something but later change your mind, let the other person know *as soon as possible* (e.g., "I've had second thoughts about what I said yesterday, and I now realize I won't be able to do this project within a month's time"). You can then go on to propose another, more practical alternative as a compromise. If some event intervenes to keep you from meeting your obligation, you also need to inform the other person *as soon as possible* and, if appropriate, offer a revised scenario (e.g., "Something came up at the office. I'll take the car to the garage tomorrow instead of today"). The crucial point is to stop yourself from getting away with *not* doing what you are responsible for.

3. *Try to work* with *a team, not against it.*

Keep reminding yourself that you *do* depend upon other people for your livelihood and happiness, and therefore that you need to remain somewhat open and accommodating to what these people may want. Whether you're on the job with your colleagues and clients, or at home with your family, friends, and neighbors, work as a team player, not as a rebel against everyone else. Get in the habit of giving, supporting, and aiding, instead of withholding, obstructing, and hindering.

4. *Do something specific that will satisfy you because it's done* your *way.*

The act of defiance in itself offers a very limited and temporary pleasure at best and inevitably involves a certain amount of pain and trouble as well. It's much more satisfying to do something *positive* to express your power—some clear-cut, tangible project over which you have total control, like writing an article, reorganizing a file system, growing a vegetable garden, or building a storage shed.

Incorporate such projects into your ongoing work life as well as your home life. You'll discover that the more you accomplish on your own, the less you'll need to defy others to satisfy your ego.

5. *Take a course in assertiveness so that you can learn better negotiation skills.*

At first, it may sound absurd: If you're so prone to defiance, won't taking a course in assertiveness make you even more aggressive? In fact, such courses are designed, in part, to make headstrong people *less* aggressive by teaching them more constructive methods of pursuing their own self-interests. Also called "negotiation" or "conflict-resolution" courses, they can help you learn more effective ways to express your concerns, elicit information, clarify misunderstandings, forge compromises, propose changes, and secure commitments.

Chapter 6

The Crisis-Maker Procrastinator

". . . __But__ I only get motivated at the last minute!"

"I work best under pressure."

Do you often hear yourself thinking or actually saying these words? If you're a crisis-maker procrastinator, the chances are good that you do. What's more, you probably take pride in this statement, as if you believed you could summon up marvelous powers of sudden courage, speed, and endurance that other people lacked. It's no wonder that when these "less gifted" people urge you to develop steadier work habits, you reply, ". . . *BUT* I only get motivated at the last minute!" Your *BUT* factor involves your fundamental sense of who you are and what makes you special.

Unfortunately, this sense of identity is only half true and almost always self-defeating. Crisis-maker procrastinators tend to overlook one very significant fact: In addition to *weathering* last-minute crises, they are also responsible for *creating* those crises. Given this fact, how much pride can they genuinely take—and how much real satisfaction can they experience—in getting out of messes they themselves helped to cause? And how does it affect their sense of self if they fail in their last-minute efforts to accomplish something important, or when they shrink from undertaking something important in the first place because they fear they might fail?

Crisis-maker procrastinators give little thought to such questions. Instead, they live by their feelings. They are addicted to the adrenaline rush of (possibly) pulling things off under emergency conditions, with chaos all around them and the final deadline staring them in the face. Their lives resemble a rollercoaster ride, sending them to thrilling highs of heroic stimulation, followed by depressing lows of lethargy or exhaustion. Like other kinds of addicts, they can't conceive of any other way to live. And also like other kinds of addicts, they delude themselves about what's fun and what's boring, what's pleasurable and what's painful, what's productive and what's a waste of time.

The hectic life of Julia, a twenty-six-year-old fashion model, reflects the overstimulated, thrill-seeking dimension of this behavioral pattern. Her motto is "you only live once," and she finds that exciting adventures are a lot more seductive, at least for the moment, than attending to the ordinary tasks of life—or to the labors involved in keeping one's commitment to long-range goals. Other people, such as her agent, wind up having to take care of her personal and professional business, while she pursues one distraction after another—person, place, thing, or mood—to keep her life dramatic and colorful.

Julia doesn't appreciate how transient her distractions really are, nor does she realize how much she contributes to the overwhelming predicaments that repeatedly beset her. Day by day, she's too preoccupied with drawing attention to herself and getting others involved in her life to take a good, hard look at the way she's wasting her own time and energy. If procrastinating over her obligations winds up putting her in jeopardy, she merely sees herself as a damsel in distress—an image that serves her melodramatic needs.

The self-destructive nature of Julia's crisis-making procrastination is particularly evident in her romantic relationships. As she puts it, she falls "madly in love with the wrong guy" over and over again.

In each case, the pattern of Julia's "mad" affair is the same. She begins by throwing herself totally into the spirit of love, exaggerating the man's virtues, focusing all her concern on him as the desired love object, and procrastinating on the other, comparatively more mundane aspects of her life, such as keeping in touch with her friends and family, paying her bills, or even attending to her career. Eventually, the man disappoints her, if only because he fails to provide her with the continually high, "crisis-level" stimulation she craves. He then becomes the target of her melodramatic hostility, which triggers a new round of emotional crises. In the end, reeling from all the romantic ups and downs she's endured, she feels horribly used by her lover or by fate. Unable to think things through beforehand, she doesn't realize, until it's too late, how much she has cheated herself by being a prisoner of her passion.

While Julia represents the histrionic, thrill-seeking dimension of crisis-maker procrastination, Sandy, a fifty-six-year-old homemaker and mother, serves as a model for the syndrome's more depressed and hysterical dimension. Her two sons and two daughters, once the source of so much drama in her day-to-day life, are now grown up, with homes and families of their own, leaving her feeling bereft and uncertain about what to do with herself.

Sandy has convinced herself that the only time she can get properly noticed or heard is when something drastic happens, so she repeatedly manufactures crises in any way she can. Granted, she's not always fully aware that this is what she's doing; but even when she *is* aware, she believes she's incapable of stopping herself or that some other person or force is inducing her to act this way.

For example, Sandy ignores household repair needs until they become so critical that they demand the requisite high-level attention of one of her sons. She puts off seeing a doctor for a health problem until it's progressed to the point where it can't help but attract the concerned intervention of one of her daughters. She sniffs out problems in her children's households and escalates them into catastrophes that, supposedly, require her crisis-management skills but that ultimately waste everyone's time and energy. And she delays making firm plans with her friends as long as she can, in order to increase their curiosity—or anxiety—about what she's going to do.

Worst of all to her self-esteem and to her listeners' peace of mind, Sandra occasionally drops suicidal statements to attract the crisis-level sympathy that she desires so much. "My life is just about over now," she says with a sigh, or "you won't have to worry about me much longer," or "What does it really matter whether I live or die?" By cultivating this attitude, she not only comes to expect an inordinate amount of compassion from other people but also justifies taking a passive, "do nothing" attitude toward her nettlesome daily tasks and obligations. Her resulting lateness, inefficiency, and nonactivity render her life even more confused and predisposed to crises, which, in turn, makes her feel even more powerless and depressed.

In a misguided effort to escape feelings of insignificance and helplessness, Sandra now drinks too much. Thus, her addiction to crisis-related drama has bred another addiction, to alcohol. Sometimes when she's drunk she simply wallows in melodramatic self-pity, but other times she gets nasty and vindictive, launching herself into an out-of-control scene that repels the people around her. Recalling these situations later, she excuses her behavior on the grounds that life has disappointed her and driven her, against her will, to do what she does. In this way, the people whom she herself has alienated are transformed into the villains who don't understand her or appreciate how much she's suffered.

Julia's and Sandy's stories provide us with brief glimpses into the two contrasting dimensions of crisis-maker procrastination: the passionate highs (more apparent in Julia's case) and the desolate lows (more apparent in Sandy's case). Now let's consider the basic characteristics that all crisis-maker procrastinators possess, regardless of the specific dimension of their problem:

1. *When faced with an undesirable task, crisis-maker procrastinators go from one behavioral extreme to the other: first ignoring the task (underreacting), then feeling intensely caught up in it (overreacting).*

   Crisis-maker procrastinators need the pressure of a crisis to get them to do a task they don't want to do. One of the easiest and most effective ways of ensuring this pressure is to put off doing the task until the last possible moment, at which point they feel compelled to apply superhuman efforts toward accomplishing it. In the meantime, they simply don't let themselves think about what lies ahead—a form of denial that, consciously or subconsciously, helps free them from feeling more responsible about it.

   Julia is very skillful at finding more pleasant things to distract her from irksome tasks until pressing deadlines make those tasks scream for attention, a situation that appeals to her need for drama. Sandy is less resourceful but equally erratic. Usually, she just sits around in an oblivious (and, sometimes, alcoholic) funk, allowing a routine, undone task to evolve over time into a suitably pressurized crisis.

2. *Crisis-maker procrastinators tend to dramatize situations, making themselves the center of attention.*

   Crisis-maker procrastinators are theatrical by nature. They want the spotlight to be upon them; and they want to perceive themselves, and to have other people perceive

them, as heroes leading turbulent lives. Procrastination is
a tool that helps them to achieve these dramatic goals: It
provides conflict (the hero vs. the dreaded task); generates
suspense (Will the hero do the task? When? How?); and
ensures an exciting climax (a tour-de-force victory or a
stunning defeat).

Julia strives to be a hero on a grand, romantic scale. Her
life is a soap opera filled with headstrong acts of passion,
including the (to her) forgivable sin of neglecting her personal duties in the name of an all-consuming love. In fact,
she's played this larger-than-life role four times in the past
seven years!

Sandy's life drama has a more somber air, befitting her
station in life. She uses procrastination to create scenes
with her family and friends in which she can star as the
noble sufferer, the long-sacrificing parent, or the tragic victim. It isn't really a character flaw that she is late for meetings, puts off repairs, fails to make doctor appointments, or
doesn't take adequate care of herself. It's the bad script
that life has given her, or the poor performance of the other
characters in the play.

3. *Crisis-maker procrastinators are easily bored and resist the
"dullness" of doing things rationally and methodically.*

Crisis-makers have trouble focusing on the practical demands of everyday life in a thoughtful, responsible, and
efficient manner because their attentiveness is geared toward a different type of stimulation: *crisis* demands. Every
other bid for their time and energy simply registers as "not
a crisis" and, therefore, "not something that requires immediate action." To go against this conditioning seems
pointless; and in the absence of any strong motivation for
doing so, they can get bored just thinking about it.

As we've already seen, Julia flits from one pleasure to

another in a deliberate effort to distract herself from having to deal with the real world. Sandy may not be as hedonistic, but she is similarly unrealistic. She can't seem to concentrate on working toward goals of a practical nature, nor can she even bother herself to keep the daily appointments she makes. She actively prevents herself from sustaining any "boring" routine of self-management by meddling in her children's lives, stirring up thoughts of suicide, and drinking herself into a stupor or a rage.

4. *Crisis-maker procrastinators feel a need to prove themselves by living on the edge.*

Deep down, crisis-maker procrastinators harbor feelings of emptiness, powerlessness, and self-deprecation. This is one of the main reasons why they need to have a heightened sense of drama in their lives; and therefore why they're so inclined to procrastinate in order to provoke drama-producing crises. Lacking a strong inner drive to accomplish most tasks, they need these crises to stir them into action. And in the absence of a healthy self-regard, they rely on these crises to make them feel like heroes battling the odds.

We see this trait most obviously in Julia, who constantly courts disaster in her love relationships as well as in her irresponsibility toward her career. It's as if she were continually trying to prove to herself that she could either pull off a miracle in the eleventh hour or else go down in flames and still survive. This daredevil trait is less obvious in Sandy because it manifests itself in a passive and more complex way—namely, in letting her household and health problems deteriorate to dangerous levels, in entertaining thoughts of suicide, and in drinking excessive amounts of alcohol.

Now that we've identified the four main characteristics of crisis-maker procrastinators by using two relatively extreme examples, Julia (the frenetic) and Sandy (the lethargic), it's time to examine a more emotionally balanced crisis-maker in greater detail. Let's consider the crisis-ridden, procrastination-filled life of my former patient Alex.

ALEX: THE CRISIS-MAKER PROCRASTINATOR

When Alex first came to see me, he was well aware of his problem and eager to change. "I can't seem to make myself do anything until I'm under heavy pressure to perform," he complained. "I'm sick and tired of living this way!"

Alex admitted that he once felt very different about his procrastination pattern. "It used to be exciting to wait until the last minute to get something done," he told me. "I felt as if I were beating the system. I could spend my time whatever way I wanted until right before something absolutely had to be done, and then I could pull it off like some sort of Superman."

This last factor—feeling like a hero—had long been especially gratifying to Alex in his professional life. He was one of many corporate lawyers employed by a large, prestigious law firm, and he welcomed any opportunity to stand out among his peers. At our first session together, he confessed:

> For years, I loved the recognition I received when I came through at the last, critical moment. The others would say, "Wow! He stayed here all night and got the job done! What dedication! Mission accomplished!" You see, *I* knew that I had to do an all-nighter because I screwed up and started too late, but usually they didn't know that, at least not for sure.

Now, however, Alex no longer enjoyed the challenge involved in putting things off, nor did he relish hearing praise he didn't deserve. He was sufficiently mature—and weary—to realize that he wouldn't truly be a hero until he ceased turning his responsibilities into pressure-bearing crises. His first step on this new, more promising adventure was to recognize his basic pattern of procrastination, not only at work but also at home, and to trace this basic pattern back to its sources in his childhood.

Procrastinating at Work

As a lawyer, Alex considered himself very ethical, reliable, and accountable. Nevertheless, he repeatedly risked disaster by letting phone calls, reports, filings, and briefings wait until the last possible moment. To save his own reputation, the firm's integrity, and, often, his client's chances, he would then be compelled to work himself *and* his staff members much harder than they would ever have needed to work if he had paced his activities more efficiently from the start.

Naturally, these episodes generated a considerable amount of friction between Alex and his staff. Spurred by the crisis that might occur if they didn't meet the suddenly looming deadline, they would all go into "work overdrive," and the result would usually be a deadline met, a crisis averted. To Alex, this outcome would be a source of pride. He would interpret the overall effort as one that "brought out the best in me and my staff" and therefore as an effort of the highest possible quality. His staff members saw the situation more clearly, and indignantly, for what it really was: a rush job that actually prevented them from doing their best and seriously threatened their morale. If they'd felt free to be honest with Alex, they might have told him, "Yes, the deadline was met, but what was so glorious about that? Aren't deadlines supposed to be met? Yes, we averted a crisis, but why did there have to be a crisis in the first place?"

Whenever a disgruntled staff member or superior did ask Alex to explain, or defend, his problematic scheduling, Alex would simply distort details to make them conform to his special sense of the truth. For example, if a court gave June 1 as the due date for a filing, Alex would consider the *real* due date to be June 30, the last day of the customary thirty-day grace period following the stated due date. If he needed to file a status report that included all case developments from April 1 to June 1, the date of delivery, he would wait until the end of May to *begin* the report, justifying his delay on the grounds that not *all* of the information was available until then.

Most of the time when Alex offered these excuses, he wasn't deliberately trying to dodge a sense of wrongdoing or guilt. He actually believed what he was saying—i.e., that he didn't have to do anything until the last moment. Unfortunately, in the mind of a crisis-maker procrastinator, the belief that you *don't have to do* something until the last moment can easily turn into the belief that *it doesn't make sense to do* something until the last moment.

On those occasions when Alex didn't have any ready justification for procrastinating, he would resort to the most primitive form of defense: he would deny or ignore the fact that a particular task needed his attention. As he'd continue doing this in his conscious mind, he'd subconsciously feel more and more pressure to act. This pressure would then begin revealing itself indirectly in moodiness, anger, and resentment, often directed at the very staff members, colleagues, or superiors whose help or goodwill he most needed in order to get the task accomplished. The result would be a full-blown situational and interpersonal crisis—just the sort of thing to get his adrenaline going so that he'd finally act!

Procrastinating at Home

Alex's wife, Patti, his daughter, Kara (age sixteen), and his son, Ted (age fourteen), suffered even more from Alex's mismanagement of time and energy than his professional associates did. For one thing, Alex allowed himself more freedom to behave as he wanted at home, which meant that he was more inclined to indulge his natural tendencies toward crisis-maker procrastination. For another thing, his family members could always tell when Alex was procrastinating in this matter, while his colleagues, staff members, and superiors often could not, either because Alex hid the truth from them or because they weren't that intimately involved in the situation.

Because Patti, Kara, and Ted had felt victimized by Alex's crises and emotional outbursts for so long, they had lost much of their respect for him. They now looked upon him as a somewhat hopeless character whom they couldn't trust to do what he said he would do. They could sense immediately when he was operating on what they called "Alex time." If he had two hours to get ready to go somewhere, he would fiddle around the house, conspicuously doing nothing, until the last possible moment, at which time he would go into a frenzy of preparation, yelling at everyone to help him and getting angry when someone didn't respond in a similarly hypercharged way.

Alex himself was usually aware of what he was doing, but he had a different, self-justifying take on it. "It's like a game I have to play," he told me:

> Some things are just plain boring to me, like cleaning up the house for company, or packing for a trip, or spending time driving somewhere. I still get a kick out of seeing how fast I can do these things, how little time I need to put into them, and the best way to play the game is to give myself the least amount of time I think I can get away with. That way, the gun is really to my head.

Alex's crisis-making procrastination also inflicted more serious, long-range damage on his family, something he didn't ap-

preciate until we'd spent several therapy sessions exploring how
he behaved with his wife and children. Instead of regularly—
and routinely—devoting his time and energy to these relationships, he would wait for some sort of crisis to arise, an occasion
for a suitably dramatic, heroic response on his part. All too often,
however, this crisis would be triggered by his own failure to meet
an obligation or by his prolonged neglect.

For example, shortly before Alex began meeting with me, his
son was caught smoking marijuana in a school bathroom and was
put on probation. Alex seized upon this crisis as a time for finally
getting closer to his son, only to discover that Ted had long been
hardened against him. He recounted the incident with a great
deal of anguish:

> I had always meant to spend more time with Ted, but it never
> seemed urgent to do it. Then he just wasn't around anymore. It
> had happened so gradually I hadn't noticed. It turns out that
> he'd been using his spare time to hang out with the wrong
> crowd—the same spare time that I had wanted to be with him
> but wasn't.

What was true for Alex's son was also true for the rest of the
family. Patti and Kara were now in the habit of making their
own independent plans rather than counting on or cooperating
with him. Faced with this alienation at home, Alex was more
and more inclined to let personal and social tasks go undone
and to busy himself, instead, with his work. Regrettably, this
meant generating even more crises in both worlds.

Learning to Procrastinate

Alex's experiences as a child and an adolescent had molded him
into the reluctant crisis-maker procrastinator he now was. His
father, an editor for the local newspaper, worked long hours,

leaving his mother to manage things at home. Frustrated by her husband's abandonment, she relied too much on her only son to bring excitement and purpose to her life. Alex had to do things her way, and every minor problem became a catastrophe. If Alex spilled a drink or tracked mud on the floor, she'd cry out hysterically, "Look what you're doing to me!"

In order to maintain a separate identity, Alex needed to create "separation crises"—in effect saying, "I'll do things my way by *not* doing them until the last possible moment." This procrastination style carried over into other areas of his life. He delayed doing his work at school and fulfilling his part of the bargains he made with friends. It was his strategy for making an adventure out of undesirable tasks, seeing just how high he could raise the stakes.

By the time Alex became a teenager, the pattern was well established: He would be almost incapable of stirring himself to act until the situation became so pressured that it would do the stirring for him. "If I didn't have any big competition in class or in sports," he told me, "I'd slack off and not do anything. There wasn't any incentive."

To add excitement to his high school life, he gambled heavily on football and basketball games. He wound up betting money he didn't have. When he lost, he had to sweat trying to figure out where he'd get it. At times, he had to be threatened with physical violence before he'd ask a friend to bail him out.

During college, he resisted gambling on games but took even greater risks in the classroom. Again and again, he would wait until the weekend before a major assignment was due to begin working on it, or he would wait until the end of the term to make up work he had never begun. True to character, he relied on other people to come to his rescue—almost always a girlfriend, to whom he had originally been attracted because she was efficient, well organized, and a soft touch.

Alex became so good at summoning up his own last-minute resources, and those of others, that he did it regularly, and somehow managed to make it all the way through law school. This achievement seemed to validate his behavior. He wouldn't let himself consider how narrowly he'd escaped failure, how much unnecessary trouble he'd caused himself and his loved ones, or how much longer he'd have the sheer mental and physical stamina to tolerate all the last-minute pressure. He simply went on with his crisis-maker procrastinator ways until these considerations were forced upon him.

Changing the Pattern

To undo the pattern of procrastination to which he was now addicted, Alex needed to reorient himself emotionally. He had to *increase* his self-motivation to get things done in an efficient manner well before a crisis situation developed; and at the same time, he had to *decrease* his emotional investment in last-minute, high-anxiety performance.

This process, like any addiction-reversal process, is a difficult one. It can't be undertaken without a certain amount of discomfort and a large amount of patience. To make sure that Alex's reorientation went as comfortably and smoothly as possible, I suggested that he develop a better understanding of his present, addicted orientation. By knowing exactly "where he was" now, I reasoned, he would be much better equipped to get where he wanted to be in the future.

To develop this better understanding, Alex kept a list in a special notebook of all the stress triggers he could identify in his current life—i.e., the situations that were inclined to provoke his crisis-maker procrastination. Some stress triggers occurred to him immediately when he sat down to begin the list; others revealed themselves only during the weeks to come, as he actually experienced them. Eventually, his list included items like "filing an important report," "helping Patti give a dinner party," "answering phone messages," "planning a family vacation," "talking with Ted about his behavior problems."

The next step was for Alex to concentrate on each item individually and list possible ways he could plan ahead to prevent a stress-related crisis. For example, his plan-ahead list regarding "filing an important report" included things like:

- As soon as it's known that a report will be due, have a meeting to inform those who are involved and to solicit their questions, comments, and suggestions.

- Within the first week, develop a practical time line for doing the report, which includes ample "extra" time for unexpected developments. Then post this time line in a prominent place and challenge myself to stick to it.

- Delegate as much of the work for the report as I reasonably can without unfairly burdening someone else.

- Obligate myself to a "midway" status meeting on the report with all involved personnel.

By combining an enhanced awareness of how he'd created problems in the past with self-generated prescriptions for the future, Alex could begin right away to feel a change for the better. This in itself was motivational. However, knowing his periodic need to feel *excitement* and not just "a change for the better," I suggested that he occasionally do something that would get his adrenaline going without his having to go through a potentially harmful crisis—something that thrilled him to think about but that he kept himself from doing out of a fear of failure, embarrassment, ridicule, or just the unpredictable.

I call this type of activity an OGT, for "*one gutsy thing*." It's anything *but* an artificial crisis manufactured out of daily events, like deliberately waiting until the last minute to get ready for work, or trying to make it home on less than a gallon of gas (challenges Alex would often pose for himself). Instead, an OGT involves a bold, positive venture into the unknown and the unsafe. In Alex's case, it meant trying out for his first role in a local theater production and, two months later, entering his first amateur tennis tournament. Through engaging in OGTs, he was training himself to look for stimulation in ways that weren't so upsetting to his home life or his career.

Alex used—and continues to use—a number of other techniques to overcome his tendency toward crisis-maker procrastination. All of these techniques, described below, are ones that you can apply to your own life for the same purpose, regardless of how severe your particular problem may be.

HOW TO STOP BEING A
CRISIS-MAKER PROCRASTINATOR

If you are a crisis-maker procrastinator yourself, you will probably find it easy to identify partially, if not completely, with Alex's problems. This identification will no doubt trigger memories of a number of specific incidents when you—and/or the people around you—suffered as a result of your time-wasting tendencies. It's important to continue this healthy process of self-realization over the next few weeks by periodically doing the following:

1. Recall at least two different occasions when you *thought something might ultimately be valuable or pleasurable to do BUT you never got started* because the prospect of starting bored you. For each occasion, ask yourself these questions:

- Why, specifically, did it seem boring to me—in other words, what particular "start-up" activities, conditions, or situations seemed undesirably tedious?
- What were the consequences of my not even trying this particular endeavor or project? How might things have been different if I had carried it through?

2. Recall at least two different times when you *finished doing something BUT wasted time, got it done late, or made more work for yourself than was necessary* because you waited until a crisis forced you to act. For each time, ask yourself:
   - Why, specifically, did I procrastinate?
   - What, specifically, was the nature of the crisis? How might I have prevented it by *not* procrastinating?
   - What were the consequences of my wasting time, being late, or making more work for myself than necessary? How did I feel? What effect did it have on my life? On my relationships?

Besides performing this kind of self-assessment every now and then, focusing on different incidents each time, you need to continue practicing new, more constructive ways of thinking, speaking, and acting. Make a sincere effort to experiment with *all* of the recommendations in each of the three following categories.

CHANGING HOW YOU THINK

1. *Practice creative visualization.*

More than anything else, crisis-makers need to learn how to relax. Trapped in their self-destructive cycles of excitement and collapse, they can't appreciate the energizing value that genuine peace of mind offers until they consciously train themselves to achieve it.

Creative visualization is an excellent tool for this purpose. It's an active approach toward harnessing the imagination and making it respond *constructively* rather than
destructively whenever problematic situations arise. The visualization exercise that appears below can be especially
beneficial for crisis-maker procrastinators because it en-
ables the user literally to feel the differences between the
"deadening" experience of sensory agitation and the "en-
livening" experience of sensory serenity.

Before trying this visualization exercise on your own,
read the directions all the way through several times, until
you feel that you can recall the general flow of the scenes
(word-for-word memory is not necessary). Then get into a
comfortable position somewhere that is quiet, dimly lit, and
free from disturbance. Many people like to lie down with
their legs straight and slightly apart, and their arms extended loosely at their sides. Others prefer relaxing in a
chair or on a couch.

As soon as you're comfortable, silently repeat the directions to yourself, as you remember them. Proceed all the
way through the exercise at a slow, relaxed pace, making
sure to allow a minute or more of quiet visualization time
between instructions. The entire visualization is designed
to last between fifteen and twenty minutes.

If you desire, you can record the directions word for word
(except for the part between brackets in number 7) on an
audiotape. You can then replay this audiotape whenever
you want to practice the visualization. While recording the
directions, speak in a slow, soothing voice, allowing at least
one minute of silence between instructions. Another alternative is to have someone read the directions to you, in the
same relaxing manner, as you actually do the visualizing.

Visualization for the Crisis-Maker Procrastinator

(1) Close your eyes and take a few deep breaths to clear your mind—inhaling through your nose, then slowly exhaling through your mouth. Now, as you resume normal breathing, imagine that you are standing in complete and silent darkness. You can't see, hear, smell, touch, or taste anything. Feel yourself getting nervous about what might happen next.

(2) Suddenly, a light switches on. You find yourself standing in a room, surrounded by the people who are currently making demands on you. You run from person to person. You see how upset each of them is, and you hear each person insist that you do something. Feel the tension increase in your body.

(3) Now, with all this chaos swirling around you, see a light switch on the wall to your left. Imagine yourself flipping the switch off and being plunged, once again, into darkness and silence.

(4) Now see something start to glow a few feet in front of you. See it continue to glow in the darkness, until you realize it's a very comfortable chair. Hear a gentle voice saying, "Sit down and relax. You are going to be soothed in all your five senses." You sit down and begin to relax. It is still dark all around the chair, but you trust what the voice has told you.

(5) Still sitting comfortably in the darkness, you hear entrancingly soft, sweet music. It reminds you of birdsong and the bubbling of springtime streams. It's the most soothing music you have ever heard. As you continue listening, you feel more and more peaceful.

(6) See the darkness around you start to lighten. You perceive that you're sitting in a lovely meadow, with colorful flowers, waving grasses, and small groves of trees. It's a bright sunny day. The blue sky has a few white clouds sailing across it, and it's the most beautiful sky you've ever seen. The fresh air smells delightful. It also feels wonderful as it lightly caresses your body.

(7) Still relaxing, feel yourself becoming hungry. Look to your right and notice a small table there, filled with some of your favorite foods [name two or three specific foods]. You start eating these foods, and they taste more delicious than they ever have before. You savor each morsel until you finish the meal, and your hunger is completely and delightfully satisfied.

(8) Continuing to relax in your chair, you notice how all your senses—hearing, sight, smell, touch, and taste—feel marvelously stimulated. Linger in your chair, enjoying this pleasant, "all-over" stimulation.

(9) Now, continuing to enjoy your newly charged senses, hear that gentle voice again, saying, "Trust that you can face whatever you need to face and do whatever you need to do without having to rush around and create chaos. Take time to enjoy life, and you'll find that tasks are easier and more pleasant to manage."

(10) Continue to relax, taking comfort in the words you've just heard. Then, whenever you're ready, slowly open your eyes.

2. *Understand that you may not feel interested in doing something until* after *you get involved in it.*

Crisis-maker procrastinators are quick to assume that a thing isn't worth doing unless the mere prospect of doing it somehow intrigues or excites them. In other words, they demand that a task or activity *lure* them into action. In this respect, they keep themselves perpetually passive—at the mercy of whims, seductions, and emergencies. Rather than actively determining for themselves what they do (self-motivation), they submissively allow outside factors to determine what they do (motivation by attraction or—in the absence of attraction—compulsion).

As a crisis-maker procrastinator, you need to coach yourself into adopting a new, more positive frame of reference. Instead of saying to yourself, "Something has to interest me before I can get really involved," you need to say, "I have to get involved in something before it can really interest me."

3. *Identify other self-motivators besides stress.*

Stress is an inextricable and essential part of life. We're inclined to think of it in negative terms, as "anxiety," "pressure," or "tension"; but in fact, it also has a positive dimension, as "excitement," "intensity," and "stimulation." Thus, in overcoming crisis-maker procrastination, your proper goal is *not* to cultivate a negative attitude toward stress or to try to avoid stress whenever possible. Instead, your proper goal is to cease relying *exclusively* on stress as a motivator, so that you don't repeatedly wind up delaying action until a crisis looms.

To do this, you need to develop a wider, more conscious variety of potential self-starters. Here's a list of possibilities to think about more specifically whenever you're faced with a task that you're tempted to put off:

- Are there ethical or moral reasons for me to do this task as efficiently and thoughtfully as I can?
- How can I make it more fun?

- How can it help family members, friends, business associates, or the community?
- How can it improve my relationshipo with family members, friends, business associates, or the community?
- How can it make me more independent or free?
- How can it educate me?
- How can it enhance my physical, emotional, or mental well-being?
- How can it benefit me financially or materially?
- How can it improve my reputation or personal sense of accomplishment?
- How can it increase my interpersonal power, authority, or popularity?
- How can it make me safer or more secure?
- How can it help me to do other things I need to do?

4. *In thinking about a task, try to focus at least as much on facts as you do on feelings.*

    As a crisis-maker procrastinator, you're inclined to *feel* at the expense of *thinking*. When faced with a task, avoid your tendency to drift from moment to moment, impulsively responding to your whims or moods. Instead, ask yourself the following questions:

- What do I need to do now, whether or not it might feel good?
- What could happen if I don't take action on this matter *now*?
- How will I feel about the situation *next week* if I don't do something now?
- How will I feel about *myself* next week if I don't do something now?

As a result of strengthening your thinking process rather than giving in so readily to your immediate feelings, you'll find that you've increased your ability to tolerate any difficulty, distress, or disinclination that you associate with the situation. This increased toleration will make you much less likely to procrastinate.

You also need to stop dismissing things that you *know* for a fact in favor of things that you *feel* might be true. Don't say to yourself, for example, "Even though this report is due Friday [a fact], I've got a hunch it won't be missed if I wait until Monday to turn it in [a feeling]." Or "I notice the gas gauge is almost on empty [a fact], but I'm pretty sure there's enough gas left to get me there without my having to stop [a feeling]."

5. *Strive toward changing your thinking style from extremist and general to moderate and specific.*

Guard against your natural tendency to confuse or "catastrophize" each new demand on your time by thinking in exaggerated terms, like "There's a million other things I have to do this week," "I'm so busy I can't see straight," "It's impossible to do this the way I've been asked to do it," or "I can't deal with this right now." Instead, concentrate on clarifying and moderating the situation by asking yourself *specific* questions, like:

- What are the most important "other things" I have to do this week? Besides doing these "other things," what could I do to at least make a step toward meeting this new demand?
- What can I do to give myself a short bit of time and space to "see straight," so that I can figure out how to manage all my responsibilities more efficiently?
- What particular aspects of the new demand make it seem

impossible? What particular aspects may, in fact, be possible? What can I do—or propose doing—to make this new demand as a whole more possible than it now appears to be?

- What aspects of this new demand might I be able to deal with right now? How can I make it possible to deal with this demand right now? If it's impossible to deal with the entire demand right now, what particular aspects of it can I handle right now? If dealing with it in any way is impossible right now, how soon can I commit myself to dealing with it?

CHANGING HOW YOU SPEAK

1. *Avoid overdramatic, polarized language.*

Crisis-maker procrastinators tend to describe things according to arousal extremes—from "incredibly exciting" "hysterically funny," and "absolutely mind-blowing" at one end of the spectrum to "unbelievably boring," "horribly depressing," and "the dullest thing imaginable" at the other end. This reflects their mistaken belief that something has to be very intense before it's worth paying attention to (and therefore before it's worth communicating).

To train yourself out of this self-destructive orientation toward extremes of feeling, try using more "intermediate" words or phrases to describe things: words like "pleasant," "amusing," and "interesting," or "difficult," "grim," and "uneventful." As you continue to avoid extremes in your speech, you'll find yourself becoming more even-tempered in general and less addicted to a crisis-related interpretation of events.

Also, remember that strong negative language tends to fuel strong negative emotions in your listener *and* yourself, whether or not those emotions are warranted. Thus, avoid saying something that may be too extreme for the occasion, like, "That's an outrageous request!" or "I'd have to kill myself working to get it done on time." Instead, say something like, "That request seems a bit demanding," or "I'd have to work hard to get it done on time."

2. *Use more "thinking" words and fewer "feeling" words.*

Making a concerted effort to communicate what you *think* about something instead of how you *feel* about it will keep you focused on responding to things more rationally and less emotionally. Instead of starting every sentence with an expression like "I feel . . . ," begin more of your sentences with thinking-related expressions, like:

- After reflecting on it, I've come to the conclusion that . . .
- Here's what I think about it: . . .
- I've decided that . . .
- Reason tells me that . . .

To attain a better balance between thinking and feeling in your speaking vocabulary, minimize your use of feeling words, such as "love," "hate," "excited," "upset," "happy," "crazy," "afraid," "troubled." At the same time, increase your use of thinking words, such as "intend," "plan," "remember," "question," "determined," "concerned," "convinced," "skeptical."

3. *Stop characterizing yourself in conversation as incompetent or victimized.*

Once you declare to someone else—or yourself—that you are helpless or put upon, you've set in motion a belief that's difficult to alter, whether or not it's really accurate. Therefore, avoid making melodramatic, self-martyring statements like "I've totally screwed this up," "This is the worst possible thing that could have happened to me," "I'm completely outraged," or "This has gotten way out of my control." Instead, talk yourself—and others—into a more positive, constructive point of view, with statements like, "I've made a couple of mistakes, but there are things I can do now to get myself back on track," or "This particular aspect of the situation concerns me, and I plan to figure out a good way to deal with it."

4. *When discussing a task or responsibility, try focusing on the positive or active, rather than the negative or reactive.*

In addition to striving not to downgrade *yourself* when you talk with others, you also need to avoid bad-mouthing your *tasks and responsibilities* so much. Anytime you hear yourself talking about what's problematic with a particular demand that's being made on your time and energy, or how that demand is affecting you negatively, shift your discussion to what's interesting about that demand, or how you might successfully manage it. Your listener will certainly appreciate the more upbeat and constructive part of what you say. Eventually, you'll get to the point where you start out conversations on the positive, active side of the situation, perhaps never getting around—or needing to get around—to the negative, reactive side.

CHANGING HOW YOU ACT

1. *Keep a record of repetitive crises in your life.*

In a daily or weekly journal reserved especially for this purpose, identify those occasions when:

(1) a crisis arose *because* you procrastinated about doing something, or

(2) you failed to address a potentially problematic situation *until* it became a crisis.

Devote a few sentences to each incident, so that later, when you reread the entry, you can easily and clearly recall what happened. Include statements about *why* you procrastinated, *what triggered* the crisis itself, and *how* you responded to the crisis.

At the end of the month, review your journal and identify two or more times when the crisis was similar in nature. Note each kind of repetitive crisis on a separate, end-of-the-month page. You will then have a list of the particular kinds of crises in your life to which you need to pay extra attention.

2. *Figure out methods for handling things so that you can avoid—or more successfully manage—recurring crises.*

Relying on the journal entries mentioned above, list on a sheet of paper all the major crises in your life that have tended to occur because you procrastinate. Then, for each crisis, write down specific positive things that you could do to avoid the recurrence of that kind of crisis, or to manage such a crisis more effectively if and when it does occur.

This activity will help you to start thinking more constructively, not only about your working patterns related to specific crises, but also about your working patterns in general. The more you can apply structure to the way you go about handling tasks and responsibilities, the less likely you are to let chaos into your life.

3. *Create your own motivators to change a boring task into a more interesting one.*

As a crisis-maker, you tend to be oriented toward fun and excitement. Why not turn that orientation to your advantage? Make a contest or a game out of a task that seems too dreary. Challenge yourself to find a particularly compelling way of doing it, or to finish it within a certain period of time. Set up some sort of special treat as a reward for a job well done.

Some of my more playful patients enjoy staging their own, personal version of "Beat the Clock," a popular TV game show during the 1950s and 1960s. In this show, the contestants were directed to work as fast as they could to complete a ridiculous task: carrying twenty-five eggs individually from one end of the stage to the other while wearing boxing gloves and skipping, for example. An enormous clock face showed the minutes clicking down to the preannounced deadline. You can apply a similar—though less ridiculous—strategy toward completing a task you don't like.

If you want to clean your kitchen before settling down to read a book, set your kitchen timer for fifteen minutes (or however long seems reasonable, with a slight "stretch" factor). Then rush around, doing as much as you can do within that period of time, trying to make sure that at least the most important things get done. When the timer goes off, stop, and reward yourself for what you did manage to do by going on to your reading!

4. *To counteract your need to stimulate yourself by creating false emergencies, engage in healthier activities that will get your adrenaline running.*

On a regular basis, do something energetic, stimulating, or daring, to feel that sense of excitement you're used to getting from crises. Run a race, dance up a storm, or gather your courage and try an OGT (see pages 185–186)!

Chapter 7

The Overdoer Procrastinator

". . . But I have so much to do!"

Over the past twenty-five years, the pace of American life has accelerated dramatically, thanks to an unprecedented increase in technological advances and economic competition. As computers and faxes are built to handle ever-greater amounts of data at faster speeds, so we are compelled to process more and more information in shorter amounts of time. As companies continue to downsize, so we are progressively forced to do the work that one and a half, two, or even three people did before. As the pool of job seekers and job jumpers keeps swelling, so we have to keep doing more to prove our worth. And as the sheer number of demands on our time, attention, and energy grows and grows, so we risk losing more and more control over what we do.

In every aspect of our life, our culture pressures us to overwork and, as a result, to feel as if we're always, somehow, running behind. Lamenting this situation, the editors of *Newsweek* magazine devoted their March 6, 1995, issue to the theme of "Exhaustion." "We're fried by work, frazzled at the lack of time. Technology hasn't made our lives better, just busier. No wonder one quarter of us say we're exhausted," stated reporter LynNell Hancock. "We need to chill out before we hit the breaking point."

Unfortunate as this dilemma is for all of us, it's especially bad for individuals who are personally predisposed to be overdoer procrastinators. These are the people who wind up saying "yes" to too many things because they lack basic skills in decision-making, prioritizing, time management, or self-assertion. Thus, procrastination becomes their indirect way of saying "no." Their characteristic *BUT* factor is: "I'd like to get it done . . . *BUT* I have so much to do!"

Overdoer procrastination can be difficult to detect. Frequently, the sufferers themselves don't recognize the personal dimension of their problem, because they can so easily blame all their time-related troubles on the "overwork culture." And to the other people in their lives, they may not look like procrastinators because they're always so busy *doing* something.

Nevertheless, overdoer procrastination is a distinct pattern of problematic behavior that can lead to premature burnout and a life only half lived. That's the bad news. The good news is that an individual can break and replace this pattern with more effective ways of functioning—ways that will ultimately help him or her to cope much better with the escalating stresses and strains that are inevitable in today's world.

Overdoer procrastination can prevent many people from realizing their most cherished ambitions. One of these people is Abby, a forty-year-old instructor of literature at a large university.

For years, Abby has planned to get her Ph.D. and therefore be eligible for a professorship, but she has always been too busy to break away. She continues to be overcommitted now, at an age that many graduate schools consider too advanced for doctoral studies. Aside from her classes, she has her student advisees, her book reviews for the local paper, her sponsorship of the school literary journal, and her arts benefit work. One job begets another, and she does little to keep herself from taking on each one as it comes. The truth is, she grasps at this extra

work almost compulsively. She hasn't allowed herself a break—
or more than a three-day vacation—since she was thirty-five.

People always know they can go to Abby, and she always feels
the need for them to come. It convinces her that she's worthy
and competent. It also wreaks havoc on her schedule. Again and
again, the pattern repeats itself: She says that she'll do something, and then she doesn't do it, or she's late, and her defense
is " . . . *BUT* I had so much to do!" She knows she needs to
slow down, yet the only way she can envision doing this is simply
to take a sabbatical and get away from it all—something she's
unwilling to do and the school would not authorize anyway.

Abby's overdoer procrastination has also kept her emotional
fulfillment at bay. She's always yearned to be married but has
never given herself the time or the psychological freedom to find
the right person, much less to become involved in a serious
relationship. Her need to prove herself through work has taken
precedence. Now she's become a workaholic—a person who de-
feats herself by working excessively, just as alcoholics defeat
themselves by drinking excessively.

Michael, a forty-seven-year-old physician, is a different kind
of overdoer procrastinator. Ostensibly, he has succeeded in realizing all of his major life goals. He has a thriving general
practice, a wife and three children he dearly loves, and a beautiful home. Underneath the surface, however, his tendencies toward overdoer procrastination have turned his dream life into a
nightmare.

Michael chose to become a general practitioner so that he
could develop close, ongoing relationships with his patients, but
his working style doesn't help him to do this. He schedules appointments every twelve minutes during office hours—barely
giving himself enough time to perform the simplest diagnostic
tests—then wonders why he's chronically running late by the
end of the day. Sometimes he keeps his patients waiting up to

three hours beyond their appointed time. When they complain, he's sympathetic, but he doesn't really take responsibility. His attitude is "My job is so demanding that my work is never done, and delays are inevitable." In other words, he feels that there's nothing he can do about it.

Michael takes a great deal of pride in being able to account for —and justify—almost every minute of his time, day after day. If he's not holding office hours, he's running to the hospital, or teaching at a medical school, or attending a medical conference. What he doesn't realize is that he *over*books his time, at the expense not only of himself and his patients but also of his wife and children.

Michael shows up for the major, preset events at home, but he misses the warm sense of continuity and communion that comes only from being a regular, active participant in day-to-day family life. He's pained by this loss, but again, he doesn't see that he is hurting himself, or that there's anything he can do to change the situation. He also doesn't recognize the sad possibility that he could be immersing himself in his work precisely in order to avoid intimacy with his family—something he does not know how to handle comfortably. Without realizing it, over-doers often keep themselves so busy that there isn't any free time to deal with troubling matters.

In Michael's mind, the dilemma is much more clear-cut and easier to accept: His work is simply too important to allow him the luxury of free time with his family. He holds fast to the belief that long hours and sacrifices "come with the territory." At times, he regrets getting into that territory, but he doesn't see anything he can do about it now, except to get out of it altogether. Since he's definitely not willing to do that, he carries on the only way he knows how: by overdoing and, in the process, procrastinating.

These two cases—Abby's and Michael's—differ in several important respects, but they each reveal the five major characteristics that all overdoer procrastinators tend to have in common:

1. *Overdoer procrastinators suffer from low self-esteem, which compels them to take on more work than they can reasonably handle.*

No matter how much they manage to achieve, overdoer procrastinators are plagued with feelings of self-doubt and unworthiness. They've persuaded themselves that they need to work exceptionally hard and long in order to feel competent. To make matters worse, despite their complaints, they're never satisfied that they're working hard or long enough. They also don't believe they can do a good job with all the work that they've taken on. Given how much work that is, their experience often bears them out!

The core of the problem is that overdoer procrastinators believe they are defined according to what they *do*, not who they are. Hence, they give very low priority to their personal or intimate needs, and ignore or deny their own feelings of discontent about the way they live.

We see this lack of self-esteem in the way that Abby makes herself so indiscriminately available to others on a day-to-day basis, at the expense of realizing her own dreams. We also see it in the way that Michael prides himself on spending every minute of his time working, rather than priding himself on who he is, or what he's accomplished, or what types of relationships he has with other people in his life.

2. *Overdoer procrastinators have trouble saying "no" or asking for help.*

To overdoer procrastinators, saying "no" seems selfish. It also goes against their desire to earn approval from others by doing things.

Asking for help is even more problematic. Not only does it have the onus of implying weakness or incompetence, but it invites possible rejection—something that overdoer procrastinators, already suffering from low self-esteem, might well find intolerable.

Because overdoers are so unwilling to turn down a task, delegate it, or ask for help, they invest too much of their own time and energy in it. Thus, they risk delaying or failing to finish at least some of the important responsibilities they've taken on.

Both Abby and Michael, for example, schedule too many daily appointments because they can't say "no" to anyone, even when it's appropriate (such as when a colleague might be available to help). The sad outcome is that instead of pleasing most people, they frustrate them, because their work overload makes them chronically late.

3. *Overdoer procrastinators tend to assume so many different roles and responsibilities that they easily get confused about priorities and distracted from specific tasks.*

The sheer *amount* of work that overdoer procrastinators create for themselves is not the only problem that keeps them from getting things done efficiently. An equally strong problem is their tendency to take on *multiple kinds* of work-generating roles and responsibilities.

It's difficult enough to sort out priorities in one particular field of endeavor: for example, to decide which job-related tasks are the most critical, or which household repairs take precedence over others. It's downright exhausting to try to establish priorities among several totally different fields of endeavor: for example, to determine whether a family matter is more important than a professional duty, a social obligation, and/or a personal goal.

Overdoer procrastinators tend to commit themselves in so many different directions that they constantly face this latter decision-making challenge. Indeed, they may have difficulty even settling down to perform a task, let alone assigning a priority to it, because there are so many competing claims on their attention.

We've seen how Abby unwittingly perpetuates this pattern. In a misguided effort to make her life full and rich, she can't resist taking on one assignment after the other— teacher, adviser, sponsor, critic—until she spreads herself too thin. In other words, she achieves exactly the opposite quality of life from what she intended!

Michael's life, too, is filled with potentially rewarding roles—doctor, teacher, husband, father—that are, instead, constantly causing distraction and confusion. The fault lies not so much in the number of roles he's acquired as in his entrenched predisposition toward overdoer procrastination. He knows there's a problem in the way he functions, but he assumes that the only thing he can do about it is to keep on *doing:* just the thing that's causing the problem in the first place!

4. *Overdoer procrastinators lack true self-discipline, especially in regard to personal needs.*

Day by day, week by week, and year by year, they passively allow the work they see in front of them to determine what they do and don't do. They seemingly can't stop working long enough to plan a better course of action—above all, one that won't bring them *so much* work. Instead, they plow ahead blindly, putting off as much as they can for as long as possible.

Sadly, some of the easiest things to put off are personal needs, the ones for which other people (presumably) are not going to hold them to account. Hence, Abby, for example, continually postpones working toward her doctorate or doing anything serious about her romantic life. And hence Michael persists in delaying any action toward making his family life or his interactions with patients more personally satisfying.

5. *Overdoer procrastinators find it very difficult to relax without feeling guilty or ashamed.*

   Because of the problematic way they live, overdoer procrastinators are familiar with, and therefore psychologically comfortable with, only two extremes of experience: charged up with work (which often leads to being overcharged) or completely wiped out. Stressful as things can become for them, overdoer procrastinators are conditioned to associate working with being "good." Usually, they can't bring themselves to stop working and "waste time doing nothing" until the pressure grows unbearable, at which point they collapse in exhaustion.

   Overdoer procrastinators frequently say they're "dying to relax," but when they do get the chance to do so, they somehow can't. It doesn't feel right. They don't really enjoy taking things easy while there's still work they could be doing, and so they let opportunities pass them by. Abby, for example, hasn't taken a real vacation in years; and Michael packs every minute of his daily schedule with work as if he actually feared being left with time on his hands.

Now let's look at a more detailed case history from my own practice that will clarify how these five characteristics are learned, perpetuated, and, if the individual tries hard enough, changed for the better. Deena, a thirty-seven-year-old office manager for a metal products firm, is a wife, the mother of two girls, ages eight and ten, and a classic overdoer procrastinator.

DEENA: THE OVERDOER PROCRASTINATOR

Deena initially came to me complaining of depression. The immediate cause was the recent death of her best friend after a prolonged bout with cancer. It soon became obvious, however, that a deeper factor contributing to Deena's depression was her long-developing dissatisfaction with the way she was living. Her friend's death was certainly upsetting enough on its own, but it had also prompted Deena to reassess her life, and she hated what she saw.

"I'm pushing myself to be Superwoman, and it just isn't working," Deena told me at our first meeting. "My friend's death made me realize that I've got to get a grip on things. I've got to make better use of my time and do what's really important, instead of trying to do everything."

Deena attributed her drive to be Superwoman to her dread that she might otherwise end up like her mother. "Mom just stayed home with the kids, and it dried her up inside," Deena explained. "I swore I would never let that happen to me. I wanted to prove to myself that I could do it all—hold down a job, keep my husband happy, be a good, nurturing mother, and have lots of close friends. But now I see that I was kidding myself. I'm doing too much for my own good!"

Although Deena's insights into this problem were especially keen by the time she came to see me, they were not exactly new. For years, she had been dimly aware that she attempted to do too many tasks and overdid many of the tasks she undertook. She couldn't help but feel drained by—and remorseful about—her chronic misuse of time and energy.

However, despite her periodic self-realizations, Deena couldn't face the problem squarely and tackle it. Too much of her pride was at stake. Instead, she had long harbored the secret, only half-conscious hope that someone else would force her to change. She revealed this secret—indirectly—during the first month of therapy, when she said:

> I strain so hard with everyone to be pleasant and agreeable all the time, but I'm miserable inside. People often tell me I handle things wonderfully, and I desperately want to hear them say that, but I sure don't *feel* wonderful about myself. As a matter of fact, I feel the opposite. I keep fearing that my husband, or my friends, or someone at work, will discover that I'm not as good as they think. It's like I'm pulling the wool over their eyes, and when they figure this out, they'll finally see what a fraud I am, and I won't be able to take it.

What Deena was describing is commonly called "the impostor syndrome," the lingering conviction, against all reason, that one is really not qualified to do what he or she is doing and that sooner or later the deception will be discovered. It's a widespread phenomenon among people who have low self-esteem— which, as we've already seen, is one of the major characteristics of the overdoer procrastinator. As her therapy progressed, the other major characteristics also came to light.

Procrastinating at Work

In discussing her job-related behavior as an office manager, Deena readily identified herself as a "workaholic," but she had a serious misperception about what that word meant. She correctly interpreted a workaholic as "a person who works too hard" but mistakenly considered the term synonymous with "high achiever" and "ideal employee."

In fact, there are big, negative differences between a superior worker—or even a competent worker—and a workaholic. For one thing, the superior or competent worker is someone who works *efficiently* as a result of managing his or her resources well, which includes allowing time and energy to do other, self-renewing things besides work. By contrast, the workaholic is someone who works *compulsively* as a result of not managing his or her resources well, which includes not spending enough time and energy on self-renewal. The former tends to meet deadlines because he or she is geared toward controlling his or her commitments and work flow in a reasonable manner. The latter tends to miss deadlines because he or she lacks this control, doing too much on one thing and, consequently, too little on another.

Although Deena was a high achiever and an ideal employee in some respects, she earned these titles in spite of, not because of, her workaholism. As she herself put it, "I work like a crazy woman. Whatever assignment I take on, I have to do everything there is to be done, whether or not it needs to be done by me, whether or not it has to be done at all!"

Deena's attitude translated into many counterproductive behaviors. She would often let undesirable assignments wait too long for attention while she overworked on more compelling, attractive, or "doable" assignments. Thus, she was frequently behind. Many times, she would labor through her lunch hour or long past quitting time, and her work would suffer from the resulting fatigue, crankiness, or hunger she'd feel. She'd frequently keep up such a frenetic pace that she'd get headaches or muscle spasms—energy dissipaters that would necessitate her working even harder when she recovered.

Summing up her job, Deena told me, "It's like having to run a race. I feel driven by machines—the clock, the phone, the fax, the intercom, the E-mail. It seems as if more and more papers are dumped on my desk, and I have to work faster and faster to prevent them from spilling over onto the floor." Her recurring theme was that she had no choice but to keep on *doing* more

and more. Office manager that she was, she never brought up
the more proactive notion of *managing* what she did.

Procrastinating at Home

Deena's descriptions of her home life with her husband, Craig,
and their two school-age daughters made it sound as stressful as
her work life. She once confessed:

> Other people see home as a place to relax. I definitely do not!
> To me, it's another place I work, and work hard. There's always
> a zillion things to do around the house. As for being a mother,
> most of the time it boils down to being on call to handle one
> problem after another. I'm so worn out by the time Craig and I
> go to bed that even sex has become a chore.

Deena's relationship with Craig was aggravated by her overdoer procrastination in other ways as well. Even on those rare
occasions when they were both well rested and had free time to
be together, Deena found it very difficult to relax and just hang
out. She couldn't resist spinning her mental wheels about the
tasks she'd already done, upcoming ones, or things she hadn't
planned yet but thought about doing someday. Often, Craig
would get annoyed by her edginess or preoccupation and go off
to have fun by himself.

Deena admitted that Craig had tried numerous times to get
her to join him in planning a saner weekly schedule, one in
which they would split household chores and reserve time for
doing things together, but that she had always refused. "There
are too many things that could wreck any schedule we set," she
told me. "I might have to work late. The kids might suddenly
need me to do something. I might be too tired. The last thing I
want is a schedule hanging over my head, something to make
me feel even more inept."

In expressing herself this way, Deena was once again revealing her rigid, self-defeating point of view that life was out of her control, that there was nothing she could do about the rat race she was running but to press herself to run a little faster. She couldn't even relax her mind enough to see the possible value of prescheduling tasks. To her, the mere act of scheduling was another task to get anxious about, and, therefore, to avoid. In fact, through a schedule may have been the last thing she *wanted*, it was the first and foremost tool she *needed* in order to improve her life.

Not having any schedule, Deena let her time at home shape itself according to the work at hand, and there was always plenty of work at hand. In giving up her time this way, she thought she was being a good wife and mother. She didn't appreciate how much she was shortchanging her husband and children by not taking the time simply to enjoy them and to let them enjoy her. She also didn't realize how much she was shortchanging herself. She once said to me:

> During the summer, when work is a bit slower, and Craig is away on business, and the kids are in camp, I do have some time to be by myself, but I honestly don't know what to do with it. I wish I could be like those people who spend all day at the beach, just sunning themselves. Sometimes it feels as if I've made working my whole life. I don't know how to just be by myself, or who I really am, or what I really want. I just know that I don't want to be on this treadmill. So many times, I feel like screaming, "Stop the world! I want to get off!"

How It All Started

Generally, overdoer procrastinators grow up never actually learning the practical skills of decision-making, prioritizing, or organizing. Some are overwhelmed with responsibility at too tender an age. They react by trying to do everything, but they don't do it very well because it truly is too much for them. Others have parents who take over all their responsibilities for them, structuring their lives so rigidly that they have little chance to gain any structuring experience of their own.

Deena belonged to the former category. The oldest of five kids, she began helping to take care of her siblings when she was only three years old. To make life easier for her mother, a timid and frail woman, she did whatever she could to fend for herself and the other children. Her father, a hardworking businessman, relied on Deena to function in this manner and praised her active, cooperative nature. "Idle hands are the devil's tool," he was fond of saying to her, while her mother would say, "I don't know what I'd do without my Deena!"

Deena grew up thinking of herself as a good *manager* of time and energy, when in fact she was merely a good *expender* of time and energy. In many respects, the net effect was the same: The sheer volume of work she could do—thanks to her youth, basic good health, and determination—made up for the fact that she didn't budget her time and energy wisely. Thus, besides helping out at home, she was able to earn good grades, excel in sports, hold a number of important offices in school clubs, and serve as a dynamic and valued volunteer in church activities.

In other respects, Deena suffered from working hard instead of working well. She often wore herself out, sometimes to the point of sickness. Feeling pressured to earn the approval of others, she rarely said no to anything anybody asked her to do. And to buy more time to work on certain things that particularly obsessed her, she procrastinated as much as she could on other things.

Deena's procrastination problem was the kind that attracted more sympathy than censure, so it was all the easier for her to ignore or deny. For example, she did complete most of her school assignments; but because of her time-wasting work habits, she would be forced to stay up long hours in the days before deadlines. When, occasionally, she did miss a deadline, she could always cite several other worthy responsibilities as contributing factors: She'd had to deal with an emergency at home, the hockey team's fund-raising banquet had been the very same week, her church had asked her to fill in for a sick day-care assistant. Because her excuse was more or less commendable, and she herself was so sincere, her teachers usually forgave her lateness, and she usually worked all the harder to catch up.

At college, Deena found that scheduling homework and study was much more daunting than it had been in high school, especially with her built-in tendency to overdo her assignments. She felt far more comfortable in the world of her part-time job as an office clerk, where busyness in itself attracted a great deal of praise and where the work was never done but was always *being* done.

At the end of Deena's third semester of college, she dropped out and entered the business world full time. Ironically, given her fundamental lack of organizational skills, she wound up becoming an office manager. The fact that she was able to survive in that capacity is perhaps the most telling indicator of how hard (rather than how well) she worked to please others.

Changing the Pattern

Before Deena could successfully commit herself to learning better organizational skills, she needed to develop a clearer understanding of *why* and *how* such skills might help her. After all, a lack of this kind of informed appreciation had previously kept her from agreeing to preschedule household tasks with her husband. Therefore, the first thing she practiced during her therapy with me was determining whether a particular task confronting her was a *priority* or a *demand*. For simplicity's sake, we used a very basic distinction:

> priority = something that is important to you, and that you *want* to do or get done
>
> demand = something that's important to someone else, and that you feel you *should* do or get done

Deena's long-range objective was to try to balance the number of priorities and demands she was handling during any one time period. If she took on too many "priorities," or "wants," many of her legitimate responsibilities and commitments would not be met. If she took on too many "demands," or "shoulds," she'd be sacrificing her own well-being, which would inevitably lead to depression, frustration, and anger.

Using this simple formula, Deena was soon able to see that she tended to take on too many demands and that some of them would have to be denied if she was going to achieve any sort of priority-demand balance in her life. Thus, for example, during a given week she might let herself agree to put in overtime at work, *or* to make Halloween costumes for her kids, *or* to help her husband set up a filing system, but she couldn't agree to do all three of these things. Otherwise, she would have no time to do any of the things that she herself wanted to do, such as study new word-processing techniques, redecorate the kitchen, or take an aerobics class at the health club.

As Deena became more mentally aware of this balancing issue in her life, she naturally began to use more organizational tools to help her exercise control over her work flow. She started keeping a daily journal, which helped her to monitor not only *how* she was spending her time but also *how well* she was progressing with certain key ambitions and projects. Eventually, she was a regular, effective, and enthusiastic user of "to do" lists, calendars, and—much to her husband's delight—household-task schedules.

If you, like Deena, are tired of, by, and from your bondage to overdoer procrastination, you, too, can learn to break free and take charge of your life. It's a matter of changing not just the ways you *do* things but the ways you think and speak as well.

HOW TO STOP BEING AN OVERDOER PROCRASTINATOR

Deena's story is but one of many that fall into the category of "overdoer procrastinator." If you scored high on the "overdoer" part of the quiz in Chapter 1 of this book, it's time for you to take a closer look at your own story, so that you can become more conscious of the particular patterns that sap your personal time and energy. Here's a brief self-assessment activity to start the process rolling:

1. Recall at least two different occasions when you *finished projects BUT spent too much time doing them or got them done late* because you did much more than you needed to do. For each occasion, ask yourself these questions:
    • Why, specifically, did I do much more than I needed to?
    • What were the consequences of spending too much time doing it, or of being late? How did I feel? What effects did it have on my life? On my relationships?

2. Recall at least two different occasions when you *wanted to do something important BUT never got around to it* because

you were too busy doing other things. For each occasion, ask yourself:

- What other things, specifically, kept me from doing that important thing? How significant *to me* was each "other thing" I did, compared to that important thing?
- What were the consequences of not doing that important thing? How did I feel? What effect did it have on my life? On my relationships?

In the future, continue to review your past for episodes of overdoer procrastination, trying to recall as vividly as possible what you did—or what you didn't do—and how you felt about it. In addition, start practicing the following guidelines, being sure to give balanced attention to all three guideline categories: thinking, speaking, and acting.

CHANGING HOW YOU THINK

1. *Practice creative visualization.*

One major reason that overdoer procrastinators find it so difficult to relax is that they think relaxation means "doing nothing"—the complete opposite of their normal "do-everything-at-once" working style. With this mistaken notion, it's no wonder they have trouble relaxing! The body can be stilled fairly easily, at least on the surface; but barring a complete loss of consciousness, the mind remains incessantly active, no matter how hard we may try to stop it.

Learning to enjoy relaxation means learning to play *with* your mind, instead of just letting your mind play with you. Practicing creative visualization on a regular basis can help you to develop this valuable ability. I developed the visualization exercise that appears on the next page especially for overdoer procrastinators, because it involves letting one's mind *rise above* entangling obstacles (or problems) in order to realize freedom (or solutions): a shift in perspective that overdoer procrastinators especially need to make from time to time.

Before trying the following visualization, read all the directions carefully several times, until you feel you can recall the basic flow of images and activities sufficiently well and smoothly without having to consult the text. It is *not* necessary to memorize each direction word for word.

When you feel you're ready to proceed, assume a comfortable position somewhere that's quiet, dimly lit, and free from distraction. Some people prefer lying down with their legs straight and slightly apart, and their arms extended loosely at their sides. Others prefer to relax in a comfortable chair or on a couch.

After you've settled into your position, silently speak each direction to yourself, as you remember it. Go all the way through the visualization at a slow, relaxed pace, allowing about a minute of quiet visualization time between instructions. The entire exercise is designed to take around fifteen to twenty minutes, with plenty of time to imagine, "see," and savor individual images.

If desired, you can record the directions on an audiotape, which you can replay whenever you choose to practice the visualization. While recording, speak in a slow, soothing voice, allowing approximately a minute of silence between instructions. An alternative to an audiotape is to have someone close to you (that is, someone with whom you can feel very relaxed) read the guidelines to you, in the same soothing manner, as you perform the visualization.

Visualization for the Overdoer Procrastinator

(1) Close your eyes and take a few deep breaths to relax
your body, inhaling slowly through your nose, then exhaling slowly through your mouth. Allow the thoughts
and cares of the day to drift away, leaving your body
light, your mind as empty as possible.

(2) Now imagine you are walking along a path through a
woods. You don't really know where you are, but you're
content to keep walking for a while because you've heard
that there's an inn somewhere ahead where you can rest
and get your bearings.

(3) You continue walking along the path, farther and farther,
until you come to a V-shaped fork, where the path splits
into two new paths. Both new paths look the same, and
you don't know which to take. Not wanting to waste time,
you proceed down one of them, but you are now feeling
uncertain as well as rushed.

(4) You continue to walk down this path, noticing that the
trees are getting closer together. You worry that you're
going deeper into the woods and won't find a place to
stay. You come to a crossroads: one path on your left,
another on your right, and a third straight ahead. All
three paths look the same, and you don't know which to
take. Not wanting to waste time, you proceed down one
of them, but you still feel uncertain and rushed.

(5) You keep walking. You turn a bend, and there are trees
in front of you, but no path. You turn around, and you
can't see the path anywhere! You realize that you are
truly lost among all these trees. Feel the tension rise in
your body as you realize this.

(6) Now tell yourself that you're going to calm down, that you're going to stop and think for a moment. Lean your back against a tree and relax.

(7) As you rest against the tree, you gaze into the woods in front of you and notice a tower directly ahead. You walk over to the tower and see steps leading upward. You climb these steps to the very top of the tower.

(8) Now, at the summit, you can see clearly over the surrounding treetops. Looking directly ahead of you, see a place where the path you were on crosses another path. Notice that if you turn right at this crossroads and head down the new path, it leads to the cozy inn you were looking for. Feel relieved at what you see.

(9) Now climb back down the tower. Feeling confident that you know where to go, walk into the woods toward the crossroads you saw. Turn right onto the new path and follow it to the inn.

(10) You enter the inn and see a comfortable chair waiting for you in the front room. You sink down into this chair, heave a sigh of relief, and relax. You close your eyes and hear a sweet voice saying, "You always have the power to take charge of your life and to see what needs to be done. Simply rise above where you are and take a good look at where you want to go." Enjoy the pride and peace of mind that these words bring you, and when you're ready, open your eyes.

2. *Say goodbye to the Superman/Superwoman myth.*

Recognize your personal limitations. Don't assume that you can always work at your peak level. Avoid thinking, for example, "I got all that work done last week, so I can get the same amount of work done this week." It may well be that last week's work severely drained your energy reserves, leaving you far less able to do a similar thing this week!

Face the fact that you can't have it all—smoothly running job, a sensational love relationship, a harmonious family life, and an exciting personal life—at least, not all at the same time. No one can. You have to expect to make choices each and every day, week, month, and year about where it is most appropriate and/or desirable for you to apply your time and energy. Just remember not to neglect any one aspect of your life for too long! The key word to keep in mind is "balance."

You also need to face the fact that you can't *do* it all. Try more delegating and asking for help. Learn to view these activities as a sign of sensible management, not a sign of weakness or inadequacy.

3. *Look at life as an adventure, not a struggle.*

To avoid staying caught in the "overwork" trap, you need to remind yourself that there can be a lot more to life than work. Repeatedly ask yourself these questions: If I had only a year to live, would I change my ways to make my life more interesting and enjoyable? If so, why not make those changes *now?*

From time to time evaluate your goals and activities in terms of how enthusiastic and fulfilled you are. When you feel that life is too hard, ask yourself: What's wrong? What's missing? What's being neglected? For most overdoer procrastinators, the answers to these questions often involve matters of relationship, heart, or spirit. Whatever your answers may be, keep them in mind the next time you are faced with making a decision about what you're going to do.

4. *Acknowledge the difference between priorities and demands.*
    Think of priorities as things that *you* consider important to do—i.e., things that you *want* to get done—and demands as things that *others* consider important to do—i.e., things that you feel you *should* get done. Making this mental distinction among tasks will help ensure that you don't spend too much of your time on one kind of task at the expense of the other.

It will also help you to develop a more friendly attitude toward time. Instead of seeing time as your challenging opponent ("I'm going to try to get as much done as I can before today's over"), you'll come to see it as your cooperative partner ("I'm going to enjoy today and use it well, doing some of the things I want to do and some of the things I need to do").

5. *Try not to depend so much on others for approval.*
    Guard against taking on tasks—or working on them until you're overwrought—simply to please someone else. Aim more toward pleasing yourself! Learn to live by the rules that make sense to you, instead of by the dictates of others. Their approval may be nice to get, but in most instances, it's not really essential to your well-being as a person.

First and foremost, you need to develop more respect for yourself by setting appropriate limits on how much you'll be available to others. This means accepting the notion that you won't always be able to do what others expect or want you to do—at least, not on their terms.

Another aspect of this issue involves not letting yourself succumb so easily to feelings of guilt or shame. Feeling bad about yourself only makes you more passive toward other people, letting their wishes control your time. It can be wonderful to do things for others out of love or respect, or to work hard for the sheer love of the work. It can only be self-defeating to do things for others to prove your worthiness to them, or to work hard just to prove to yourself that you're a "good" person.

6. *Focus your thoughts on how you are going to gain control over things, instead of how things are controlling you.*

In a sense, this is the "bottom line" for overdoer procrastinators—thinking in terms of being the master of your life instead of the victim of your life. Much of your day-to-day anxiety and fatigue comes from believing that you're at the mercy of other people and events, a belief that's bound to foster self-pity, despair, resentment, and anger. The more you can think of yourself as the one who is responsible for—and capable of—organizing your day, the more competently and joyfully you'll go about doing so.

CHANGING HOW YOU SPEAK

1. *Don't hesitate to say "no" to others when it's appropriate.*

Saying "no" more often (especially at those times when you're definitely thinking "no") will not only help you to establish priorities and set more reasonable limits on your time and energy expenditures; it will also help you to build character. In effect, the more you learn to say "no," the greater value your "yes" will have.

Recognize the fact that there are many types of "no," from the blunt "no" (such as "No, I won't do it"), to the polite "no" (such as "No, but thanks for thinking of me"), to the "no" with an explanation (such as "No, I'd like to go, but I just don't have the time"), to the "no" with an alternative (such as "No, I won't be available to drive you today, but if you still need a ride, I'll have time next Tuesday"). Give yourself the freedom to use any type of "no," depending upon the situation.

2. *Replace your "I should"s with "I want to"s.*

Overdoer procrastinators generally express themselves in terms of what they *should* do instead of what they *want to* do. This habit only reinforces their sense of passiveness, both in their own minds and in the minds of their listeners.

Pay attention to what you say to people, and begin to create an impression of being in charge of your own destiny. For example, instead of saying, "I *should* be getting back to my desk to work," try saying, "I enjoyed our talk and now I *want to* get back to my desk to work." Over time, you'll wind up doing more things that you want to do, and you'll develop a greater sense of control over your life.

3. *Talk more about your options than about your obligations.*

Overdoer procrastinators need to avoid using their conversations to gripe or plead for sympathy and, instead, use them to generate helpful suggestions. In your conversations, this means focusing on the *goals* you want to accomplish and then soliciting input from others, rather than focusing on the *work* that's bothering you and then simply sounding off about it.

For example, let's suppose that there's a committee meeting that you dread attending but feel you have to attend in order to express some ideas. If you want to bring up the subject to a friend, don't just say, "I have to go to this awful meeting" (work-oriented). Instead, say something

226   **It's About Time!**

like, "I want to communicate my ideas to the committee members, and I'm wondering how I can do that without going to this meeting" (goal-oriented).

4. *Speak less defensively, and more positively, about the times when you're not working.*

   Overdoer procrastinators tend to feel guilty or ashamed when they're not working, saying things like, "I wasted a lot of time last night doing nothing." Try not to make such apologetic, self-deprecating statements. Instead, look for positive things to say about nonworking times, like, "I thought about all the things I might do on my vacation" (rather than "I just sat around daydreaming"), or "My wife and I talked and caught up with each other's lives" (instead of "I just hung around the house with my wife").

5. *Avoid characterizing yourself in self-talk in conversations as powerless or overwhelmed.*

   Don't say things that cast you as a victim, like "I'm swamped with work," "I'm so busy I don't know which way to go," "I have no choice in the matter," "This work is killing me," or "There's nothing I can do about it." These offhand remarks can easily turn into self-fulfilling prophecies!

CHANGING HOW YOU ACT

1. *Keep a journal of everything you do during the day, so that you can evaluate your use of time.*

   For a certain period of time (at least two weeks, preferably a month or more), record at the end of each day everything you did. Then, at the end of each week, review all that you've written. As you review, ask yourself these questions:

- What activities were important to me?
- What activities were important to others but not really to me?
- What activities could I have skipped doing?
- What activities did I spend too much time doing?
- What activities did I *not* do that were important to me?
- What activities caused me the most stress?

This kind of review will help you to see more clearly what choices you need to make so that you can work more effectively and derive more personal enjoyment from your life.

2. *Make—and follow—daily "to do" lists that are organized to help you make good use of your time and energy.*

Either the night before, or first thing in the morning, list *all* the activities that you have in mind for the coming day. Don't forget to include leisure time activities, especially ones that involve enjoying the important people in your life. Then, after you've finished your list, go back over it and do the following:

(1) Eliminate those things that you don't really have to do or want to do.

(2) Put a star next to those things that are important or urgent. If you run low on time and energy today, concentrate on the starred items and skip the rest.

(3) Put an "R" next to tasks that are routine, such as exercising, grocery shopping, going to the cleaners. Then look at all your "R" items and ask yourself, "Is there a way of saving time on these or making them more fun?" You might decide, for example, to go to the grocery and the cleaners in one trip instead of two (saving time), or

to exercise to music (making a routine item more fun and less stressful).

(4) Put "PO" next to those things that you keep putting off. Then be sure to save this list after the day is over. If you don't do these things today, you can do them, as well as "PO" items left over from other days, on a special "PO" day that you devote to getting all of these items out of the way!

(5) Reconsider those tasks that are going to take a lot of time without many compensating benefits. Ask yourself for each task, "Is it really worth doing?" If your answer is "no," cross it off. If your answer is "yes," ask yourself, "Is there any way I can shorten the time, or do *part* of the task today and the rest later?"

(6) Consider what is missing from your list. Make sure, for example, that you have at least a few activities that are going to be fun, personally enriching, or restorative to your spirits. Overdoers tend to neglect these activities and suffer for it!

(7) Do a final review. Ask yourself, "Am I overdoing it today? Have I left myself any extra time for the unexpected (including unplanned breaks, distractions, possible emergencies)?" As a general rule, it's wise to allow a twenty percent margin of unscheduled time per day (not in one block, but in increments throughout the day) to accommodate the unanticipated.

3. *Plan to incorporate an ample amount of leisure activities into your life.*

Besides doing relatively small things each day that are nonwork-oriented, such as taking a walk, calling a loved one, or practicing your golf swing, be sure to plan more elaborate leisure activities in advance: vacations, season tickets for the theater, participation in the softball league, an adult education course, a special evening out with your partner or family. Once you've scheduled these activities, you're not likely to skip them—and enjoying such activities on a regular basis is vital to your emotional well-being.

4. *Enlist or hire help whenever appropriate.*

Overdoer procrastinators are highly resistant to seeking help, and yet their failure to do so is one of the things that hurts them the most. If you can't afford to hire help, barter for help. For example, if it takes you long, hard hours to do computer work because you're inexperienced, see if you can get someone who's an expert to help out in exchange for your doing something that you do very well. If you can't delegate an entire task, delegate parts of it. Also, make a habit of brainstorming for time- and energy-saving ideas among your family members, friends, and business associates.

5. *Create contingency plans and "backup" systems before you need them, so that they're readily available if and when you do.*

Whenever you're making plans to do something, try to think of some of the things that might change or go wrong. Be sure to make at least tentative plans for handling each of these possible occurrences, so you won't be overwhelmed— and delayed—by the unexpected. Also, be sure that you've set up specific resources (or "backup" systems) to help you save time and energy if a change of plans or an emergency arises: for example, an on-call baby-sitter, a potential replacement secretary, a stock of frozen microwave dinners, a home supply of overnight-mail envelopes.

6. *Learn to take relaxation breaks as needed and to enjoy un-expected free time.*

Each day, take time during stress-filled situations to remove yourself briefly for a breather. This will ultimately "buy" you more time, because you'll be more refreshed—and efficient—when you return to each situation. And when you suddenly get some free time dumped in your lap, relax and savor it. Don't just look for more things to do. If you feel restless at first, don't give up the idea: You'll be surprised at how quickly you can learn to take things easier! If you are still having trouble relaxing on your own, enroll in a meditation course or biofeedback program.

Chapter 8

The Process of Change

Perfectionist

Overdoer

Dreamer

Worrier

Crisis-Maker

Defier

Right now, you have a good idea of what specific changes you need to make, based on the guidelines you've studied for overcoming your particular styles of procrastination. But how does the *process* of change actually occur? Assuming you are making an honest effort to change, what can you expect to happen over the next few days, weeks, and months? How can you help to guarantee that you will persevere and that you will succeed in realizing all the new goals that you have set for yourself?

The answer to these questions lies first in understanding the various stages involved in making a transition from a negative lifestyle to another, more positive one. Second, it lies in learning how you can keep yourself motivated and on track, despite discouraging moments.

THE STAGES OF CHANGE

There are three basic stages of personality-style change:

1. The "On Your Mark" Stage: from denial to awareness

2. The "Get Set" Stage: from awareness to commitment

3. The "GO!" Stage: from commitment to making it happen

The first two stages are preparation stages. The third stage is the one in which you will be most ready to change the ways you speak, think, and act, according to the guidelines described earlier in this book.

Generally, people who engage in a self-change program proceed through each of these stages in sequence. Few self-changers, however, make *consistent* progress. Don't be surprised and don't give up if, despite a good start, you find yourself drifting backward from time to time. Do be prepared, however, to motivate yourself at such times so that you resume moving forward as soon as possible.

We'll consider the issue of keeping yourself motivated later. Right now, just remember that two steps forward and one step backward means that you're still ahead of the game! Now, let's get a clear picture of each of the three stages of change.

1. *The "On Your Mark" Stage: from denial to awareness*

Denial is a *pre*-change or *anti*-change stage, in which you don't even recognize that you have a problem. For some people, the blindness is a willful effort to avoid assuming responsibility. For others, it's a true lack of realization. Either way, you're more focused on what's *outside* you than on what's *inside* you.

When you're in denial, you may be experiencing difficulties because of your procrastination, but you put the blame for the trouble elsewhere. If others suggest that you have a problem, you defensively—and reflexively—view *them* as the problem: they're hassling you, they don't understand, they don't know what they're talking about. You may occasionally feel moved to change, but it's most often because of some external pressure, such as the threat of losing your marriage or your job.

To help yourself move through your denial, you need to become more conscious of yourself, so that you see your life situations more clearly in terms of what *you* do and who *you* are. Reading this book has been a significant start!

2. *The "Get Set" Stage: from awareness to commitment*

Once you acknowledge that you have a procrastination problem, you may still not be ready to change your ways. You may be *getting set* to change by imagining what life would be like if you didn't procrastinate, by discussing self-help strategies with others, or by reading books and magazine articles on the subject. But you may remain ambivalent about actually committing yourself to change.

In many respects, the "Get Set" Stage is the most critical one of all. You can stay in it indefinitely, seesawing back and forth between desire-for-change and resistance-to-change. Or you can finally begin that most dramatic and valuable transition in the entire process of change: the steady progression away from ambivalence toward a serious commitment to change.

Ambivalence is characterized by indecision, frustration, and cross-purposes. Although you wish you could be rid of your problem, you're not quite ready to establish any personal goals so as to deal with it. Perhaps you assume that you can just learn to live with the problem more graciously, without having to do anything about it. Maybe you think that sheer awareness of the problem will eventually cause it to go away on its own. Possibly you harbor the secret hope that something magical will come along to banish the problem—a new love, a better job, a financial windfall, or a sudden creative breakthrough.

During the "Get Set" Stage, you rely heavily on *BUT* factors to explain your lack of initiative: Yes, I'd change, *BUT* I'm too lazy, *BUT* it's too hard, *BUT* I'm afraid, *BUT* I've got too many other things to do, and so on. These help you to save face as you rationalize why change is impossible. The more you catch yourself using these *BUT* factors in your thinking and speaking, the more evidence you have that you are still ambivalent about change.

Another sign of ambivalence is saying to yourself, "Yes, one part of me wants to change, *BUT* another part doesn't." This kind of thinking indicates that there are several "selves" inside of you that are having difficulty living in peace. At times, you may feel as though an internal war is waging between your child self ("I want to play") and your adult self ("I want to meet my goals"). Or perhaps your insecure self ("I can't do it") is battling with your competent self ("Oh, yes I can!"). Or maybe the fight is between your lazy self ("I'm a couch potato") and your energetic self ("I'm rarin' to go!").

Pay close attention to these dueling dialogues and, instead of letting them run their destructive course, turn them into peace negotiations. Each of your selves deserves attention. You need time to play *and* to work, to acknowledge your insecurities *and* to give yourself pep talks, to be lazy *and* to be dynamic. When you can allow all of these parts to have appropriate space in your life, according to your best, conscious judgment, they will learn to co-exist in a more balanced and comfortable manner. As a result, you will no longer feel so paralyzed by ambivalence. You can then move with more freedom toward making the changes that will help you overcome your procrastination pattern.

Regret is another issue that keeps many people stuck in indecision and resistant to change. Regret can be useful if it teaches you a lesson that you can apply to the future. However, regret can be harmful if you waste your time and psychic energy bemoaning the past instead of living in the here-and-now. For example, a woman who blames her perfectionist procrastination for contributing to her divorce may fixate on thoughts like "If only I had been less wrapped up in my job and paid more attention to my ex-husband, we might still be together." By continuing to focus on her regrets, she avoids changing her perfectionistic patterns *here and now,* so that the same type of mistake is less likely to happen in the future.

Regretting is easy. Changing is more difficult. In the fantasy world of regret, doing something differently is a breeze. In real life, it can be terrifying. Whenever you regret something that happened—or did not happen—because you procrastinated, you are mourning a loss: a better possibility that did not get realized. If you sincerely want a similar possibility to come true in the future, your only recourse is to let go of the regret and start working toward that possibility *now.*

Here's how to turn regret into positive movement toward change:

• *Let your regrets be self-educational.* Learn from your past—don't just regret it. Some people use thoughts of the past to avoid changing. Their credo is "This *was* so; therefore, this *is* so and *will always be* so." It is true that the past influences the present, but healthy, growing people don't keep themselves stuck in the past by simply repeating what they regret. Instead of wallowing in your regrets, study them to find out more about what is truly important to you.

If, for example, you often regret not spending more time with your children (or your parents), you have strong evidence that you need to reorder your priorities. If you find yourself repeatedly regretting the loss of your youthful enthusiasm for life or the fact that you never kept up your painting, take it as a sign that you need to

allow yourself more time and space for fun or creativity.
If you continually regret not having done a top-quality
job on a work assignment, it may well be a clue that you
really do need to put more thought and care into your
work.

• *Use regret to inspire change.* We'll be looking at a number of different kinds of change-motivators later, but let's
consider the value of regret as a call to do better, instead
of merely another form of self-punishment. The mottoes
"Never again!" or "I'll show everybody!" can be great
energizers, pushing us to transform our lives.

Therefore, don't use regret just as a means of complaining. Use it as a basis for thinking, saying, or doing
things differently, so that whatever you regret doesn't
bother you again. In other words, turn your images of
regret into catalysts for change.

Lianne, a former dreamer procrastinator, used her regrets about not going to college at age eighteen to prod
herself into going to college at age twenty-eight. Recently
she boasted to me:

> I no longer complain about what happened to me. In-
> stead, I look forward to what I'm doing about it. Sure,
> sometimes I still think it would have been nice if my
> parents had encouraged me to make something of my-
> self and not be such a princess. But you know, if they
> had, I might have rebelled. I can't keep faulting them
> for not steering me into college. I know one thing for
> sure. If they had, I wouldn't have the feather in my cap
> that I do now!

• *Anticipate future regrets before you make decisions.* Before acting on impulse or habit (such as partying instead
of getting your work done), give a few moments' thought

to what could go wrong and how you'll feel about it later. Then, you can determine a course of action that will at least keep future regrets to a minimum. People who normally make decisions without considering what could go wrong often feel overwhelmed with regret if and when things don't work out.

In addition to regret, a related issue that keeps people from changing is *guilt*. Like wallowing in regret, nursing guilt is a way of acknowledging the need for change without actually doing anything constructive about it. Those who do move beyond their guilt toward positive change discover a wonderful bonus: their guilt begins dissipating and may even vanish altogether.

Ralph, a former defier procrastinator, commented:

I rarely feel guilty now. I don't put off doing things out of spite. I'm stronger now, so I don't need to be resistant to prove myself. I'm more responsible, so there's much less guilt to deal with.

When I was a chronic procrastinator, negative thoughts about what I wasn't doing kept crowding my mind, but that didn't mean I'd get off my butt. I was too exhausted torturing myself with guilt and resentment to do anything but watch TV, or fiddle with my fishing gear, or drink beer.

These days, my mind automatically fills up with positive thoughts instead of negative ones. I think of what I *have* done, instead of what I haven't done, and what I *can* do, instead of what I won't do. This gives me a whole lot more drive to actually go ahead and get something done!

Ralph's shift of mind-set from negative (guilt ridden) to positive (action oriented) is a prime example of progressing beyond ambivalence about change toward commitment to change. Essentially, this movement is the turning point in the whole process, when the procrastinator finally realizes that he or she not only has the capacity to change but also the self-obligation to change. At last, the *BUT* factors have less power as the procrastinator comes to appreciate that, in the words of the eminent eighteenth-century English philosopher Samuel Johnson, "Nothing will ever be attempted, if all possible objections must be first overcome."

3. *The "GO!" Stage: from commitment to making it happen*
The "GO!" Stage is the crucial one in which you actually conquer your procrastination habit. You appreciate that the time for change is now. You realize that you need to make positive changes in three areas: thinking, speaking, and acting. You're eager to move forward, even though you know it will be a struggle.

• *Thinking positively.* It all begins with the mind. Alter your attitude and you take a giant step toward change. Your mind can make almost anything happen if only you focus on the possibilities, letting the objections take a backseat.

At age forty-four, Carol thought she was too old to go to college. "By the time I graduate, I'll be almost fifty," she lamented. "Well," replied her positive-thinking husband, "then there's no time to waste. You had better enroll today."

Think positively and you will be able to speak and act courageously. Eleanor Roosevelt expressed this beautifully when she said, "You gain strength, courage and confidence by every experience in which you really stop to look fear in the face. You are able to say to yourself, 'I lived through this horror. I can take the next thing that comes along.' You must do the thing you think you cannot do."

To help yourself think more positively, practice the guidelines for "Changing How You Think" that apply to your particular procrastination styles, as identified earlier in the book. By absorbing these guidelines until they become second nature, you'll begin to think more creatively and optimistically about yourself and all the things you want to accomplish. You'll develop a "can-do" attitude that will build your self-confidence and self-esteem.

Unfortunately, it is quite possible to linger halfheartedly in the thinking mode of change without moving much beyond it. Dreamer procrastinators, for example, with their predisposition to live in their imaginations, are especially susceptible to this kind of stalling. Whether or not you're a dreamer procrastinator, your thoughts need to be reinforced and extended by speech and action, or else they remain nothing more than fantasies.

If you find yourself stuck in the thinking mode of change, periodically review the chapters in the book that deal with your procrastination styles. This activity will serve as a "reality check," helping you to progress beyond idly envisioning change to actually saying and doing change-related activities.

• *Speaking positively.* The language you use in self-talk or speaking to others also makes a profound difference in how you view yourself, your life, and the specific tasks that lie before you. Bear in mind that words do not just *describe* situations, they also help to *determine* situations. By giving expression to your thoughts, you're taking a stand, making yourself more likely to accomplish what you've set out to do.

Speaking positively reinforces your ability to think and act positively. You create a language of change that inspires commitment and action (e.g., "I'm learning

to . . . ," "I'm planning to . . . ," "I have done . . . ," "I
can do . . .") rather than doubt and passivity (e.g., "I don't
know how to . . . ," "I won't . . . ," "I haven't done . . . ,"
"I can't do . . .").

For more specific help in speaking positively, consult,
reconsult, and, above all, practice the guidelines for
"Changing How You Speak" that apply to your particular
procrastination styles. We all had to learn to talk before,
when we were toddlers, so that we could achieve our
growing-up goals. Now, we need to learn new, improved
ways of speaking—so that we can achieve our adult goals.

Most important, listen for your *BUTS!* Do you hear
yourself repeatedly giving voice to *BUT* factors to explain why you're not doing something? Here are two examples of *BUT* factors:

> I really want to get a new job, *BUT* it's so difficult for
> me to update my résumé (a classic sign of dreamer
> procrastination).

> I could get this report done now, *BUT* I like to wait
> until the last minute (a classic sign of crisis-maker
> procrastination).

If you do hear yourself vocalizing *BUT* factors, try
these two transitional strategies to prevent your *BUT*
statements from becoming your final say:

Strategy #1: Change your placement of *BUT:* Put the
negative part of your statement *first,* and the positive part
of your statement *last,* so that you end on an upbeat,
change-oriented note. For example, the *BUT* factors expressed above could be better rephrased as follows:

> It's so difficult for me to update my résumé, *BUT* I
> really want to get a new job.

I like to wait until the last minute, *BUT* I could get this report done now.

Strategy #2: Start turning your *BUT* statements into *AND* statements. In motorists' language, it's like substituting a green light for a red light. Thus, the original *BUT* factors cited above are transformed into:

I really want to get a new job, *AND* it's so difficult for me to update my résumé.

I could get this report done now, *AND* I like to wait until the last minute.

In making this shift from *BUT* to *AND*, you have acknowledged that you have *two* issues to consider: The negative one no longer simply cancels out the positive one. Thus, you can go on to figure out how to resolve the implicit conflict. With practice, you'll soon discover how smoothly you can add a resolving *SO* statement:

I really want to get a new job, *AND* it's so difficult for me to update my résumé, *SO* I'll get my friend to help me.

I could get this report done now, *AND* I like to wait until the last minute, *SO* I'm going to make a start now, then make a final review of it at the last minute.

Although speaking positively takes you one giant step further toward change, you have to be careful not to sabotage yourself. Many people live by their word, and so they find the journey from speaking to acting a fairly smooth one. Others are not so fortunate.

Every type of procrastinator has a certain amount of trouble matching words with action, but some types experience added difficulty. Dreamer procrastinators, for example, who are inclined to confuse fantasizing with doing, are especially likely to say one thing and do another.

So are passive-aggressive defier procrastinators, who have an ingrained, self-defensive strategy of agreeing to do things that they have no intention of doing.

Make yourself more aware of any difficulties you personally tend to have in doing what you say you'll do. For example, you may often suffer a crippling lack of self-confidence when it finally comes to doing the action you've promised; or you may routinely rationalize away any discrepancies between what you say and what you do; or you may have a habit of speaking impulsively, assuring action before you've really given thought to what you will or won't do. Work to change these discrepancies, and you'll be amazed how your words will begin to translate into deeds!

• *Acting positively.* When energy is obstructed, tasks, even simple ones, can seem heavy and burdensome. But when you free the flow of energy, the very same tasks that seemed so onerous can be stimulating, even fun.

Marie, a "natural born" worrier, drained herself of energy by overplanning, overhoping, overthinking about whatever she had to do. By the end of the day, she had done nothing much, but needed to rest, feeling exhausted. These days, her energy is no longer blocked and she enthusiastically directs it toward accomplishing whatever she wants to do. Now, when she rests, it is with a satisfied feeling of fulfillment. And as the next day begins, she looks forward to realizing new accomplishments, viewing herself now as a "natural born" achiever.

Your best means of acting positively is to practice the guidelines for "Changing How You Act" that apply to your major procrastination styles. The more frequently, conscientiously, and ambitiously you weave these actions into your day-by-day existence, the faster, more significant, and more satisfying your progress will be.

As you progress, however, you are bound to experience occasional seductions or relapses into your old, self-defeating habits of procrastination. Perhaps you'll flounder during a "slump" period in your life when it's hard to do *anything* constructive, much less strive for a personality change. Or possibly you'll take on too much, too fast, or something too difficult, making some sort of breakdown inevitable. Or maybe an especially challenging situation will come along that will upset your equilibrium, and, as a result, throw you off your reform program.

In such situations, the key to remaining in the change process is learning to regard the setback as temporary, not conclusive. Don't waste time feeling guilty about it, but do revitalize your commitment to change.

Alex, the crisis-maker procrastinator profiled in Chapter 6, described a particularly positive way that he's developed to recover from a relapse:

Whenever I get stressed and regress to my old ways, I try to learn from it. What disturbed me so much? How can I prevent it from getting to me the next time?

I usually learn that what stresses me the most is feeling like things are out of my control, that I'm being victimized. At that point, I need to restore my sense of self, so that I can realize that I'm a competent, effective person despite how the stressful situation makes me feel.

The last time I was going through a particularly bad period, I made sure one day to act the opposite of a victim. I went out and bought a new CD I've been wanting. And as I sat back and enjoyed the music, I was able to recall the many good choices I've made in my life. It helped reassure me that I could make good choices in this troublesome area as well.

The goal during any period of relapse is to start moving forward again as quickly as you can. Bear in mind that even a small step in the right direction helps.

Sonya, a former perfectionist procrastinator, testified to this truth:

> When I'm emotionally distraught or exhausted, I'm certainly not at my best, and that's when I make mistakes or give up. The difference now is that I accept the fact that I'm not always perfect, rather than fighting against that fact.
>
> Fighting just takes up too much energy! I use whatever energy I do have to begin getting back on track. I focus on little steps, easy stuff, things that offer immediate comfort—like buying a pair of shoes I need or returning a phone call to a friend. When I start taking care of these things, the other, bigger things start falling into place. I've taught myself a lesson: Even in the lowest valley, I can still see the top of the mountain, and know that I'm going to get there eventually!

The process of change can take months or even years, as you persevere in reinforcing, solidifying, assimilating, and preserving various change-related thoughts, speaking patterns, and behaviors. The beauty of the process is that as you get accustomed to accepting change rather than fighting it, change itself just keeps on getting easier, more enjoyable, and more gratifying.

You can help yourself go through this process successfully by using the entire book as an ongoing resource: rereading it, underlining what's pertinent, starring what you've accomplished, and continually making the book's messages more personal to you. As anyone who's involved in mental development will tell you—including therapists, teachers, meditators, athletes-in-training—the more time that you spend thinking constructively about something, and the more ways you can personally relate to what you're thinking about, the greater, more potent impact those thoughts will have on your life.

When you are in the "GO!" stage of change, you will experience a self-transformation. Thinking, speaking, and acting positively will become a more natural part of you. You will eventually feel like a new person, and your old, procrastinating ways will seem alien. Whether or not you can imagine exactly what this liberation will be like for you, have confidence that it will happen, just as I've seen it happen for so many other hard-core procrastinators. As Shakespeare wrote, "We know what we are, but know not what we might become."

MOTIVATING YOURSELF
TO STAY ON TRACK

By now, you may be well aware that changing your procrastinating ways is necessary or at least desirable. You may also be very clear about what you need to do to change, and what the process of change entails. But how do you actually *make* yourself change?

Forcing yourself to change by self-imposed orders, threats, and punishments is not the answer, although it may, on occasion, get you started—or restarted—when you're really stuck. The key to a lasting transformation lies in motivating yourself to *want* to change, so that you gravitate toward ways of becoming a new and better you, like a flower turning to the sun for nourishment.

Here's how to inspire yourself to continue on the path to change, no matter how discouraged you may feel:

- *Identify, and repeatedly remind yourself of, the reasons why it's good for you to change.* It helps some people to recall particularly difficult experiences they had as a result of their procrastination, as mentioned in the section about regret. You can also—or alternatively—remind yourself about specific occasions when you triumphed or felt great because you did *not* procrastinate, or because you utilized one of the guidelines for overcoming procrastination. Other things to remember are:

  - dreams or goals that depend upon your changing
  - the well-being or good opinion of your loved ones
  - any positive image of yourself—perhaps from the past, perhaps imaginary—that you want to actualize in the future
  - any personal heroes (real or mythical) that you'd like to emulate

  Write a list of these reasons and be specific, so that you'll have something tangible and vivid to look at when you need inspiration. Display the list in a prominent place—like your refrigerator door—so that it's easily accessible. And keep adding to this list as you think of, or experience, new reasons.

- *Play a game with yourself called "Avoiding Avoiding."* As I said in Chapter 1, procrastination is essentially an un-resolved or only partially resolved approach-avoidance con-flict: You want or need to do something (approach), *BUT* for some reason you don't (avoidance). The "Avoiding

Avoiding" game is a way of challenging yourself, in a positive, adventurous way, to enact the *approach* part of the conflict despite your simultaneous pull toward *avoidance*.

For example, let's suppose that you're tempted to procrastinate because of the following fear-based *BUT* factor: "I'd like to ask these people for their advice, *BUT* I'm too intimidated by them." Instead of leaving things there, invite yourself to play "Avoiding Avoiding." Recognize that you do fear talking with these people, allow yourself to feel this fear, but go ahead and talk to them anyway. In doing so, you're sure to gain a certain amount of courage and competence, which will lessen your fear in the future.

"Fake it till you make it" is a phrase many procrastinators use to help themselves stay focused on *approach* rather than *avoidance*. I recommend that you, too, use it as you experiment with new, non-procrastinating behaviors. You *can* fool yourself as well as others into belief, as Anna did in Rodgers and Hammerstein's *The King and I*, when she whistled a happy tune as she marched forward into a new country she secretly feared.

• *Make the most of any criticism you get.* Criticism of what you've done or said, or about who you are can be devastating, *if* you let it be. This is especially true when you're in the process of changing your ways and, therefore, extrasensitive to other people's reactions. Bear in mind that you do have a choice: You can either let the criticism hurt you or you can let it help you.

To do the latter, think of criticism as a training device. When someone says something negative about you or about what you've done or not done, consider their words or behavior as nondefensively as possible, so that you can perhaps learn something about your weaknesses, deficiencies,

or misjudgments. Then, make a point of working with what
you've learned. It will be easier for you to do this if you
can ignore any general, negative reflections on your character (such as "What's wrong with you?") and focus, instead, on specific criticisms (such as "Every day this week
you've had to race around to get to work on time").

As you continue to treat criticism this way—the same
way that a professional athlete must treat criticism from his
or her coaches in order to improve—you'll develop what
Ron Goodrich, senior psychologist at Bellevue Hospital in
New York City, calls "self-muscle." Self-muscle is the
"me" power that allows you to withstand outside criticism
and other forms of stress, and to become all the stronger
for having successfully lived through them. We are not born
with self-muscle. We acquire it by "working out" situations
that are difficult for us, rather than running away from
them. As you build self-muscle, you acquire psychological
strength, emotional resilience, and high self-esteem.

Bill, the former defier procrastinator profiled in Chapter
5, developed a great deal of self-muscle simply from alter-
ing his response to criticism. By teaching himself to use
criticism as a motivator for change rather than allowing it
to trigger his anger, he transformed himself from an emotional weakling into a powerhouse of self-control:

> I used to be very defensive about criticism because I used
> to get it in a very destructive way. As a kid, I got put
> down a lot. I was screamed at and told I was lazy, stupid,
> would never amount to anything. It got so I'd believe it,
> and I'd shout right back, "Okay, this is who I am. Take
> me, or leave me!" The circle of attack–fight back never
> stopped.
>
> Now, I look at criticism as potentially useful feedback.
> I can find out what's working and what's not, what's caus-
> ing resentment or confusion in others (whether or not I

intended it to) and what's apparently okay. Of course, I'm not exactly pleased by criticism, but I accept it much, much better.

Sol, a former overdoer procrastinator, also built up strong self-muscle by using criticism constructively rather than destructively. The most valuable after-effect for him was that other people no longer seemed so threatening:

> I don't let people harass me or intimidate me. I just say "yes" or "no" or tell them I'll get back to them later, instead of always saying "yes" and then not following through because I was sorry I'd said "yes."
>
> What's more, I sometimes even ask people I respect to critique what I've done, something I would never do before, and what they have to say has been surprisingly valuable. I've also learned to give criticism to others in a way that's well received. It's all a matter of taking the time to listen to people, and to think before I say something, or do something, that I might regret.

• *Reward yourself for progress.* In addition to patting yourself on the back when you've effectively completed a task, followed a guideline, or received a compliment, try giving yourself a specific reward. This will ensure that you let yourself *experience* your accomplishment, and, therefore, that you develop positive sense-memories to associate with being successful.

One way to create an ongoing reward system is to develop the habit of doing your work *before* you play. Jeff, the former dreamer procrastinator profiled in Chapter 3, spoke highly of this approach:

> When I was a procrastinator, I did all the fun things first, then I'd work—if I ever got around to it! These days, I make sure to do the work first. It's been great for my

output, because this usually means doing it early in the day, when I normally have the most mental and physical energy. Also, I'm much less likely to get sidetracked while I work because I know it will delay the fun. For play, I always have energy, especially when I know I've earned it!

Jeff added that he hasn't let himself become fanatical about always putting work before play. Occasionally, while he is writing down his priorities (something I specifically advised him to do to overcome his procrastination habit), he realizes that a certain play activity takes precedence over a specific work activity. He told me:

> Sometimes I'm not sure what to do first. So I say to myself, How will I feel about myself after it's over? For instance, will fixing the faucet make me feel better about myself than playing tennis? Tennis, after all, helps me to stay in shape—another one of my goals. If I put off playing tennis, will I feel resentful, which will hinder me from doing other work? Or if I put off fixing the faucet, will I feel so guilty that I'll hate myself and get hell from my wife? Asking myself these kinds of questions, I might well decide to play tennis first and fix the faucet later.

Another, more targeted way to reward yourself is to promise yourself a special treat for having accomplished something in an effective manner. Here are some treat suggestions:

• Keep a running "reward list," containing items that you'd especially like to buy yourself. Then, choose one item from this list *in advance* of doing a task or meeting an obligation as a reward to give yourself when you're done. That way, it can serve as an incentive. Your list could include clothes and accessories, hobby gear, concert or game tickets, art objects, anything tangible that tickles your fancy!

• Plan to go out for a special meal. This could involve trying out a new restaurant, visiting an old favorite, or having an especially elaborate picnic in the park. If you wish, invite someone special to join you. Be sure to tell them the occasion! Sharing your sense of accomplishment will help reinforce it.

• Plan to go to a movie or to rent a movie you've always been meaning to see. Or plan to go to a concert, a play, or a museum. Again, consider sharing the experience—and the reason for the experience—with someone special.

• Plan to do something that will make you feel physically wonderful, such as engaging in your favorite sport, getting a massage, taking a long walk in the woods, or spending an afternoon in your hammock. The association of physical pleasure with feeling good about yourself will continue to stimulate the change process.

• Plan to attend a special class or workshop—one that you've long been interested in attending or one that catches your eye in a catalogue. The more new skills you acquire, the more skillful in general you'll become, including your efforts to overcome your procrastination habit.

LIVING WITHOUT PROCRASTINATION

When patients first start telling me about their self-defeating habit of procrastination, many of them admit that they worry about the *solution* almost as much as the *problem*. They're afraid that giving up procrastination will eventually mean a life with a great deal more hard work and considerably less freedom to goof off. If this picture of life without procrastination were true, why would anyone ever want to change?

In fact, the real picture is very different, and downright inspirational. My patients who have successfully overcome their procrastination all report that their new quality of life is far better, and more personally liberating, than they would ever have imagined. Here's what they most often have to say about their new life without procrastination:

- *They feel happier and prouder about who they are.* Their tendency to procrastinate eroded their self-respect, causing them to doubt their own sincerity, integrity, and capability. The resulting guilt and shame they felt seriously undercut their potential to enjoy themselves. The actual process of breaking their procrastination patterns helped them to develop a stronger, less constrained, more exuberant self-regard. And their subsequent, non-procrastinating lifestyle keeps on nourishing that improved sense of self.

  Joan, the former worrier procrastinator profiled in Chapter 4, remarked:

  I trust myself more these days. I've stopped second-guessing every move I make. My fears no longer paralyze me. Sure, I still feel frightened sometimes and question whether I can really do something, but when it comes, it's only a temporary feeling. I can now put my concerns into perspective. When I feel my fears start to overpower me, I shift my focus to my strengths and do something physical to renew my energy, like dance, jog, or stretch.

  Morgan, a former crisis-maker procrastinator, also spoke to me about his newfound sense of self-worth:

I trust myself more, and I can appreciate who I really am, all on my own. I don't feel I have to create a crisis to fix or rush to be the hero anymore. My life today is much saner and much less chaotic than it used to be.

- *They feel better about doing things that need to be done.* As procrastinators, they automatically dreaded or resented many of the tasks confronting them, regardless of the particular nature of those tasks. Any call to work represented another problem and another high possibility of failure, given their entrenched tendency to misuse their time and energy.

As non-procrastinators, they're less anxious about, and more open to, tasks. They accomplish more, and they relish more of what they accomplish.

Karen, the former perfectionist procrastinator profiled in Chapter 2, described this feeling as follows:

I am more enthusiastic about so many things! I really don't work harder, just smarter and with more vitality. Not fighting procrastination, I find things much easier to do.

I used to get frenzied and run around like a chicken with its head cut off, getting little done for all the fuss. These days, my flow of energy is great because I manage it well. I feel less drained, more alive. I do things as they come up. If one day I feel sluggish, or low on time, I just think about what's most important to take care of *right now,* and I do it.

- *They experience more respect from—and toward—others.* Living under the curse of their own self-generated procrastination, they caused a great deal of frustration and pain to the people around them, especially those who were closest to them. Inevitably, many of their family members, friends, and business associates were forced in self-defense to assume the role of critic, taskmaster, or even opponent. The procrastinators, in turn, became counterantagonistic, thus alienating themselves from the very people whom they most needed for support.

Living without procrastination, they have reformed this situation, winning back the confidence and high regard of the people around them. Thus, they are newly able to appreciate what these people have to offer.

Evelyn, a former defier procrastinator, made the following comment about her reformation:

> It's obvious that people find me more agreeable today than they used to, and I can't tell you how gratifying that is. The biggest difference is with my husband, Ed. When I became a new person, so did Ed. Just as I am now more dependable and likable to him, so he is now to me. It's been the single most validating thing that could have happened. With my procrastination in check, we have more of a life together.

Heather, a former dreamer procrastinator, confided to me how much her world had opened up since she'd changed:

> Once I finally got a grip on my time-wasting habits, I quickly developed a great group of friends, really positive people. It's as if I somehow magically turned from a repellent into a magnet. They let me know in all sorts of ways that they believe in me. I rely on their belief in me to get myself started.

• *They feel more control over their use of time.* When they were procrastinators, they often had trouble focusing on tasks, were easily distracted, and viewed themselves as victims—rather than masters—of time. Now, after surmounting procrastination, they have more of a sense of command over their lives. It's easier for them to concentrate on tasks and to accomplish them within suitable time periods.

Leonard, a former worrier procrastinator, admitted to me:

> I used to take so much time to do something that was really quite simple. I'd dilly-dally with it. Then I found that if I'm really psyched, the same thing would take me just a few minutes. It's Parkinson's law: Work expands to fill the time you give it. So now I make less time available, give myself a firm deadline, and it works much better. I recognize that what I do doesn't have to be the best, just good enough. I've developed a much keener feeling for what's good enough. And that makes me feel a whole lot more powerful than before.

• *They live a life that's more harmonious, balanced, and fulfilling.* Prior to getting rid of their procrastination patterns, they constantly lived on the edge. They were never sure whether they were actually going to start—or finish—all the things they wanted or needed to do. Perhaps they could get through the day without feeling pressured, confused, scared, or defeated. Perhaps they couldn't. Maybe things would work out okay in the long run. Maybe they wouldn't. They might manage to keep things going in their life, but deep down they felt as if they were going nowhere. The world they inhabited was one they could never be sure of.

Now, free from procrastination, they live in harmony, flowing with the natural rhythms of their life. They create order instead of disorder. They feel buoyed by faith in themselves and the future, and excited by the opportunities they have to exercise their decision-making and task-performing skills. They are sure that they're progressing in directions they want and need to go, instead of being pushed and pulled in several different directions at once.

Deena, the former overdoer procrastinator profiled in Chapter 7, reported:

> For the first time in my life, I am making realistic choices. I make sure to put quality time into what I value. My goals are now within reach—not too few, so I won't get bored, and not too many, so I won't get anxious. When I do get stressed, I don't give up or panic. I take a couple of deep breaths, relax, and then continue at a slower pace. I keep reminding myself that I don't have to do it all.

Like Deena, Leonard, Karen, and the other former procrastinators profiled in this book, you, too, can create a better lifetime for yourself, instead of allowing your life and time to keep on killing each other. First, it's a matter of realizing that what you do with your time, and how you experience what you do, *is*, in fact, your life. Then, it becomes a matter of living the best you can, so that you can accomplish what's important to you. After all, It's About Time!